PRAISE FOR THE BOOK

Neil has a unique way of simplif

approach to contracting is a great e.

appraisal of the highs and lows of contracting, and a clear guide on how to setup and what it will take to make it work if you choose to follow in his footsteps. I did and I haven't regretted it.

Hazel C

A great read! - This book is a good introduction to contracting. It is very comprehensive, wide ranging, easy to read, very logical and information. I wish I had had all this information in one book, when I gave up my 'permie' job many years ago.

I would highly recommend this to anyone, whether you are thinking of entering the contract market, are new in or are an old hand, this book helps you quickly grasp the important aspects of the move from 'permie' to contractor, plus for those old hands, provides the latest information on IR35 etc, etc.

Greatly recommended!!!

Ross M

I've known Neil for years and know that he has always been frustrated by the lack of information to help people move into or get the best out of contracting.

Finally, he's got round to creating this short yet comprehensive book, setting out what you need to know. It's well structured and peppered with examples and checklists to help you consider key issues such as personal priorities and commercial practicalities.

And for the experienced contractor? I've learned from it and I've been successfully contracting for over a decade!

Well worth a read.

Derek A

DEDICATION

To all you budding contractors....be brave...break free!

ACKNOWLEDGEMENTS

There have been a few selected people who have really helped me with this book. The inspiration finally came from Siobhan Kirby one evening over dinner – about the 50th dinner where I'd taken someone out to explain 'how to go contracting', golloped my food down, or worse, not eaten any because I'd been talking all evening. It took Siobhan to say, 'you know, this is great and I feel really inspired to think about contracting as an option, but why don't you write a book about it – you know so much!' And that was the inspiration.

I would sit on the train on the way back to Oxfordshire from London and bang out chapter after chapter. I got a good draft of the first section and passed out to some trusted friends - Derek Allan, Luke Vilain, Ross Martin, Julie Ferguson, Hazel Collins, Paul Roberts, Caroline Andersen, Heather Graham and James Brookner.

Together these people have helped me with the basics of the book, read the manuscript and been with me on the journey as we headed towards publication. Their feedback has been invaluable – I even took notice of some of it! Joking! Rob Bradley – my accountant – from Castle Tax and Accounting Services helped with the tricky tax sections – I had many a head scratch trying to pull those pieces together!

My wife, Dawn, (www.dawngoudgedietitian.com) who helped with the 'looking after yourself' section of the book.

And finally, the dynamic trio that was the Launch team. Starting from a chance meeting sitting next to a bloke on a flight to Kos, who just wouldn't shut up. Turns out he's Nigel Morgan, my social media guy (www.morganpr.co.uk), who I didn't realise I needed until 3 hours later on that flight! Nigel convinced me that I needed to 'get out there' on LinkedIn and Twitter and Facebook (all those things I know nothing about really!) in order to promote the book properly. Nigel was the link into James Bishop (www.proactiveweb.co.uk), who created the website at www.breakfreegocontracting.com and to Helen Stothard (www.hlspublishing.com), who has been instrumental in sorting out the formatting, some missing sections in the book, the front and back cover and the Kindle and print versions of the book. A phenomenal team, without whom, this book would still be an aspiration. They made it real.

Finally to my wife and children who've had to put up with my mad cap ideas over many years but this one was one that just had to happen. They've listened to me go on about the book as it has gestated over the year that it took to write.

Contents

INTRODUCTION

You've picked up this book for one of many reasons. You've had that nagging doubt about working in a permanent role and you wonder if the grass is greener working for yourself. You're coming back to employment, maybe from a career break or maternity, and thinking, could this be for me? Graduates, you're wondering if you can make it straight into the contract world (and the answer is YES YOU CAN!). You're from overseas and you want to understand the UK contract market and how it works and how to break into it.

You know contractors or you've seen contractors floating about companies and you know they get paid a lot more than you and yet, they're not that good. Someone may have given you the 'good news' – you're no longer required and suddenly you're faced with a lot of different options, one of which is to go it alone, work for yourself and go contracting. There will be many different reasons.

So, what's stopping you? For most people, it's the fear of the unknown. A myriad of questions surface. Am I really good enough? Am I really the right kind of person? Could I cope? What is it like really on the other side? What are the risks? How do you go about setting up a company?. How do you go about getting a contract and how do you handle agencies? What am I worth? All this sounds quite frightening

I was amazed to find that there wasn't a book that dealt with all these questions. Sure there are books out there that drill down into contracting and they're very good. What I thought was missing was a book written from the perspective of a person entering the contract market and answering all the questions that I had and have had since becoming a contractor.

I made the move into contracting over 10 years ago and it was the best thing I ever did. My background is that I trained as an engineer with Rolls-Royce Aerospace, blowing up jet engines in the development department for a number of years. I then went into consulting with PA Consulting and Ernst & Young, working mainly with Aerospace and Defence companies. These were all great companies to work for and gave me a great experience in breadth and depth. So I knew a few things about project management, change management, process improvement and had a number of tools in my kitbag.

My last consultancy assignment was at Boots Healthcare International, integrating Clearasil for them world-wide and they converted me to a permanent employee. I had a great time as a Change Programme Manager with them for a couple of years and then things changed and I was no longer needed. I had a choice to try something new- I looked at property development quite seriously but chose to 'stick to the knitting' – carry on with what I knew best, which was project and change management.

So I have been through what a number of you will be or have experienced, moving into the contract world, into the unknown, doing what I thought was best, talking to people and trying to build up a network. Looking back, I did okay, but I could have got to where I am now a lot quicker with the guidance you'll find in this book.

I've made this book a practical guide to all the things you will need to think about as you embark on this new and exciting chapter of your life. But it should also appeal to existing contractors.

There are great tips and advice as you go through the book that anyone who is already in the contracting market should know. After all, you can always improve your interview techniques, your CV, the way you handle clients and agents and possibly most importantly, understand how you can get roles that really will enhance your day rate. It will also help you understand if you're on the right tracks to make that move into contracting.

In summary, this book will help you:

1. Understand all the things that you as an individual need to consider in order to work out if contracting is a real option for you

2. Understand the practicality of becoming self-employed and the steps you have to take to set up an appropriate Business

3. Gain inside knowledge of the process to get into your first contract and subsequently how best to manage yourself on a client site

4. Maximise your day rate as you progress in your contracting career

THE CONTRACTOR MARKET PLACE

Before we get into all the good stuff about you, your CV and agents, it's important to put your mind at rest about the current and future state of the contract market, the market into which you're considering moving. In a few words, the contractor market in the UK has been growing steadily and is forecast to continue growing.

The Current State of the Contracting Market in the UK

There are currently about 4.2 million self-employed workers in the UK according to the Office for National Statistics (ONS), about 14% of the overall workforce or, put another way, 1 in 7 of people who are in work are self-employed! There are around 1.5 million people who are contractors or freelancers (according to the PCG and Kingston University). All of these people have made the choice to get into contracting – why? While 25% of people have been forced into contracting by being made redundant, 75% of people move from a permanent role into contracting because they realise it's a better place to be. The main reasons are:

- **Financial** – contracting pays more than the permanent market

- **Avoiding Corporate Politics** – contractors don't avoid this but there is significantly less politics and even if there is and you don't like the environment, contractors can just move on

- **Active control of career progression/increased Job Satisfaction** – people often get fed up with being promised promotion, expanded roles and new challenges only to find that they often don't transpire. In the contracting world, how fast you rise and how much you earn is largely dictated by you

- **More flexible working** – contractors have much more flexibility over when they work. It just depends on how much you need to earn.

You may identify with some or all of these reasons to move into contracting. I went contracting for a number of these reasons. I enjoyed my job but didn't enjoy corporate politics; I've always wanted to run my own business and I knew very well that my salary wasn't going to rise as quickly as compared to going contracting.

Eurostat labour force data from 2011 estimates that 23m people across Europe are freelancers or contractors. The contracting market in the UK is the largest in Europe, according to a survey by Freelance Professional Services (FPS), and it is expanding. It grew by over 14% between 1998 and 2008 (according to data from the PCG and Kingston University) and has continued to grow by 11% between 2008 and 2011. Sure, the market changes depending on the economic climate and sometimes there is more demand than at other times but in a recent survey (November 2012), the Recruitment and Employment Confederation (REC) found out that 81 per cent of the 600 companies that they surveyed in the UK said they would be maintaining or increasing agency workers over the next year.

Furthermore, there was a boost in the number of temporary staff who were subsequently taken on as permanent employees with almost one in four temps landing a permanent role this way, the highest transfer rate since the survey began in July 2009.

When are Contractors needed?

Company Expansion - When companies want to expand, often they cannot get the resources they need quickly enough, so employing contractors makes sense. In this situation, companies often embark on big infrastructure projects or major reorganisations to make themselves more efficient for the future. Some permanent employees, who have the potential to rise, are given the opportunity to lead these projects and show what they can do but it can be quite difficult to pull all the required staff out of the line positions they hold to work on a project, which by definition, has a start and an end date. So companies see it as a logical move to bring in specialist skills to be part of their big ambitions.

Company Down-Sizing – Even when companies are down-sizing, there are opportunities for contractors. Companies will often dismiss permanent staff (to be seen to be achieving targets) and then employ contractors, who don't appear as permanent headcount. Companies will be looking to run projects to make themselves more efficient, so they can do the work they need to do with fewer people. This can mean re-designing their work processes, implementing systems that allow them to run operations in a more automated and cheaper way, or, favourite for some years now, off-shoring, where work is moved to a more cost effective country such as India or the Philippines and outsourcing, where work is parcelled up and given under contract to another company. So, whichever way the market goes, up or down, there are opportunities for contractors.

Company Efficiency - Even when companies keep their headcount level, they will still want and need to stay competitive and to do this, they need to become more efficient – that is get more from the people they already have, more bang for their buck if you like. Contractors are a great option in this situation because they represent a more flexible solution for companies in that they can hire contractors to do a specific project and then get rid of them again at the end. So even when the market is static, there are opportunities for contractors.

In fact, in a survey conducted in 2012 by contractjobs.com, the report concluded by saying that the economic downturn had actually been good for many contract workers.

What do Contractors earn?

On average, a contractor earns £52,820 a year compared to £26,000 for a permanent employee (survey by Market Storm Global). However, it is important to take into consideration that a contractor may not work for that entire year. By nature, contractors move from role to role and some may not be in contract for a full year.

For many people, the thought of being their own boss seems tempting; however, on average, 40% of freelancers work more than 41 hours a week, 15% put in even more than 51 hours per week. One in four freelancers take no annual holiday and of those who do, 45% continue working while on their get-away.

The Future State of the Contracting Market in the UK

Given the current rate of expansion, it is very likely that the market will continue to expand. In the future, companies are going to need more and more flexible workforces, reducing reliance on the numbers of permanent staff, which means more and more contractors. Redundancy has become a fact of life now and many people will consider contracting following redundancy as a potential move for them as they realise that being permanently employed isn't the safe and secure option that they expected.

I firmly believe that in the future most people will contract and companies will have relatively few permanent employees. Why? Well because employing people is a pain in the backside. The laws now are becoming restrictive, employees are placing more and more demands on employers, the red tape around employing people means more and more people have to be employed to manage employees; there's pensions that are now compulsory, National Insurance to pay, tax to manage and pay, benefits to manage and on and on…

The plus side is that companies can make a serious amount of money by employing people. The top 10 FTSE 100 companies make £900,000 per employee per year and even if you take out the distortion caused by BP and Shell, the top 8 companies make almost £390,000 per employee. So employers want to keep this bit quiet. They want you to work for them. They want you to work for a decent but relatively small amount of money compared with what you could get by contracting. They want you to stay forever, so that you become so much part of the fabric of the company that you really would find it difficult to go somewhere else. I refer to this as the "fur-lined rut" – it's just so comfortable, you're never going to get out!

People are scared of being sacked, of losing their jobs – fear introduced by companies. Redundancy is a dirty word. Or they're hanging on for that golden handshake that may or may not be realised – in reality, these are golden handcuffs!

BUT there is coming a point where the maths won't stack any more. Gone will be more and more of the big monolithic companies, enter stage left, the new, nimble, agile, internet savvy, socially connected, multi channel companies. They will set up and last a few years while they exploit a particular niche in the market, then move on. They will want an ultra flexible work force, where ONLY contractors will be accepted. Get ready. It's going to happen.

The future will be about a complete shift in emphasis. The power will shift way from employers to an emerging independent workforce – an extension of what we call contractors today. The independent worker will move away from "what can I do for this company?" and shift to an attitude based on "what can this company do for me?" The future will be about "Brand Me" – my brand, how can I improve it, what additional skills can I get or what skills do I need to move to an area I'm more interested in or that will give me better rewards, a better standard of living or a better work/life balance.

If a company does not offer this, then the independent worker will move on and find a better match. Interviews will be conducted the other way round. The independent worker will have a beauty parade of potential employers, conducted via video link, often simultaneously, where employers place their bids in front of the independent worker, who can then evaluate the balance of the offer versus the level of improvement in their skill set and how quickly they can achieve this new goal in their life. Of course, once the independent worker has achieved their goal, the employer will become of less use and the next round of bidding will take place.

Employers will have to become more savvy about what they are good at and improve what they're not good at in order to attract the most talented people. They will have to be constantly improving their processes, be at the cutting edge or even 'bleeding' edge of innovation in order to make it an interesting place to work – one where independents gain the most value and need to have that company on their CV.

The Competition

So who are you up against in this market place? It ranges from other contractors to small consultancy firms right up to the big consultancy firms. As a contractor, you sit at the bottom of a triangle that has the Big 4 (Deloitte, PwC, IBM and Accenture) at the top, a myriad of middle market or boutique players, with annual turnovers down to a few million, then it's you and me and a few million independent contractors. It's a huge market just in the UK (£9bn annually!) and there is plenty of work to go round. Good consultancy firms are constantly sold out, good contractors are never available, they're always in demand.

So the main competition comes from contract firms, other contractors and consultants.

Competition from Consultancy Firms

It's a good idea to know about how the big consultancy firms work so you can keep an eye on what they're up to. They can be your best allies, but they can also be the people who put you out of work! See the Appendix for more information on how the big firms work.

In most cases, you will come across the big consulting firms and, in most cases, you will get along fine with these guys. So how on earth can you as a lone contractor hope to compete against these boys and girls? The answer lies in the fee rates charged and you demonstrating that the difference between what they provide and what you provide isn't really worth the difference. Smaller consultancy firms have good success when clients realise just how much they are spending (or have spent!) and when they realise that actually, the guys the big firms put on the ground are not that special.

So how does this come about? Clients think they are doing themselves a favour by negotiating with the big firms and driving down the price of the consultancy engagement. In fact, what happens is that the partner in charge has to go back to the office and work out how they can deliver the work for the price and quality and still maintain the profit margin that all the big firms have (approx. 40%!). Inevitably, the thing that gives is that they have to put more junior people on the engagement in order to make the profit margin target. And this is a risk. More junior people need more management attention, they need on the job development, they are often slower to ramp up and can be very green (new) to the consultancy world.

In my roles working with some of the big firms, I've had people come straight from training, landing in the account, reporting to me, where a conversation might go along the lines of, "So you know about project management then do you?" Reply from the spangly new consultant, "Er, well, yeah, we covered that, like, on the third morning of training, I think!" – Trust me, it happens. So don't put the big boys up there on too much of a pedestal. They have their fallibilities too.

So your job is to, quietly, or noisily, get on with your job, deliver excellent output and become very embedded with the client, to the point where they can't really do without you. When the big boys are around, be wary. As I said earlier, they can come in and take over an entire department and one of the first things they often do is look to replace the contractors with their own people. If you are good AND they like you, you may get a stay of execution. In which case, watch out for them putting one of their team alongside you and bleeding you dry of all the good stuff that you know. They **can** lure you in and spit you out!

On the positive side, the smart thing to do is to see if you can get yourself in with them. Work with them, prove your worth and get them to see that you are not a threat but a useful resource. Once on the inside with these guys, you can do very well. They will often take you with them on to a new project (if they are allowed to use contractors) and it can be a hugely beneficial relationship. Your rate usually benefits – your charge rate is likely to be significantly lower than the rate they charge the client for a similar level of resource and they may find it is possible to get you on board, brand you as one of them and charge you to the client at a margin that makes it profitable for them. And you get their multi-million pound brand on your CV.

Competition from Smaller Firms and Other Contractors

The smaller firms will be hoping to increase their 'footprint' in their clients by introducing more of their team. Agencies will want to place more contractors. So the competition for placement can be quite intense. In every company that I've worked in as a contractor, there has always been a liberal spreading of big consulting firms and smaller firms, who are often niche players – they specialise in one particular area or set of skills like Business Analysis or Project/Programme or Change Management. It is more and more common these days for big clients to have a Preferred Suppliers List (or PSL). The idea is that all these consulting firms have to go through a 'selection' process, often run by the client's procurement team. This gives procurement the opportunity to ensure standards are appropriate and that rates are consistent across similar suppliers. So you can hear consulting firms talk about a 'rate card', which is literally a list of rates that they are allowed to use for certain specified roles. This has now been extended to agencies who offer contract resources – they have to satisfy procurement and have to work within certain specified rates.

The reason for explaining this is because when you go in to a client, if you go through an agency or consulting firm, they will only have a certain amount of flexibility that they can offer you on rate, before they cease to make their required margin. Equally, if you can get friendly with the people who run the smaller consulting firms, it is again a way of getting a good rate, because they will undoubtedly have negotiated higher day rates than the agencies can ever hope to.

Sometimes the big firms will cut their rates in order to get a foot in the door on a particular project and then expand gradually and introduce more expensive consultants later.

As an independent contractor you can assume that there will be plenty of competition in every client you work for. All roles will increasingly be fought over by a number of potential resource providers. You must do a great job but also be aware of other agencies, contract companies and consulting firms. They are competitors but they are also a potentially great source of further work.

WHY MAKE THE CHANGE AND BECOME A CONTRACTOR?

Flexible working and contracting is the future and if you want to be part of it, it will pay to start now. Those still left in the current model will find it very difficult to move out of their roles and adapt to the new ways of working. If you're already there, you will be used to change, used to moving around and used to being flexible.

Talk to most contractors and they will tell you that losing their job or moving on from the fur-lined rut was the best thing that ever happened to them. They have broken free! Free of the constraining shackles of employment, of bosses hanging over them tracking their every move, criticising, being politically motivated, keeping them down in the organisation and getting in the way of progress.

Contracting can be extremely liberating. You can work when you want – within reason! – as long as your day rate will stand it. You choose which contract you go into and which company and industry you want to work in. If you don't like it, you have the choice to move on.

I have worked in Aerospace, Defence, Pharmaceuticals, Media, Fashion, Banking, Healthcare, High Technology. I've worked in the UK, Hong Kong, America, Poland, Spain, France, and Germany. You get to choose! It can be up to you.

I'm an engineer by training. One of the best examples I can think of in my time as a contractor is standing in the world's largest newspaper press hall in Broxbourne **inside** the press, with the red ink still oozing off the rollers after the first print run of the evening of The Sun. I thought, "Who the hell else is going to get an opportunity like this?"

I have been a contractor for the past 10 years. In that time I have had virtually no down time away from a contract. Throughout that time, the market has risen and fallen, rates have fluctuated, contractors have been thrown out of companies en masse and still, I have only had 3 weeks where I couldn't find a job immediately – and that was very early on in my contracting career. How? Well it takes a good deal of planning, networking and plain old luck on timing. We'll cover this in more detail later but one thing you will come to realise is that where you end up, on which contract and for what company is largely down to timing.

I had a great example recently where I had a few days between contracts and had a call on a Friday evening from one of the agents in my inner network. He called me and cajoled me into a contract for 2 weeks just to help him out. We tussled on rate for a while, then I agreed. On the Monday morning, I had already arranged a meeting with another agent. They then proceeded to offer me a job for £100/day more for 6 months! I had to turn it down as I had already given my word and in this game, once you've said "Yes" to a contact, even verbally, that's it. It's a done deal and you cannot go back on your word, even for more money. It can be as close as that. As it happened, I ended up staying on the first contract for 9 months. Sometimes, fate intervenes and deals you a hand you weren't expecting but there is no point mulling over what might have been. Part of making your own decisions is that you stick to them and manage the consequences.

I've been in a situation very recently where I was about to leave a contract and had wound up my network to let them know. I had three offers arrive simultaneously, all really very good roles, all with slightly different flavours of challenge with them, all about the same rate. The thing that decided me in the end was the guy who phoned me up was the MD from the consulting firm that wanted me. We negotiated a rate on the phone and he put me on the spot there and then – "So do we have a deal?". You can't say, "Oh, just wait a minute while I phone all the other guys up". No, it's your choice, you weigh it up and stand by it once you've made it.

I manage my contracts so that, in most cases, I go from one contract on a Friday into the next one on the following Monday. It's my choice. I know plenty of contractors who work for 9 out of 12 months and take 3 months off for a break between contracts. That's their choice. All the contractors I know are happier than they were and earn more money than they did in their permanent roles.

The point is that contracting can be whatever you need it to be to suit your circumstances.

Contracting is all about CHOICES and TIMING

So you're not alone in this brave new world that you're looking to move into. It is a well trodden path. What this book sets out to do is to give you the ammunition to be a good contractor. Armed with the relevant information and an understanding of where you're good and where you could improve.

It has taken me 10 years to get to this point. I've learned a lot along the way. I'm about to share this with you. I have helped many people get on to the contracting ladder and it was only recently that one of my buddies said "You should write a book about this, because you make it all sound so straight forward, you understand how it all works and you've inspired me to make the leap!"

Reading this book will help you, no doubt. But talk to other people. Talk to your nearest and dearest. Talk to your friends about it. Don't just take my word for it.

There are risks in making the decision to go contracting. Hopefully, what I'm about to tell you will help you minimise those risks. In the end, it is going to be your decision. Only you can decide if the risks for you are worth taking.

WHERE TO START – SOME BASICS

There's a whole bunch of things that you can do that will help you figure out if contracting is for you. I'm going to take you through a series of important questions so you can understand who you are, where you're trying to get to, understanding what you are (your "brand"), then some things around making sure you have the best CV that you can, understanding your "network" – the people you already know – and then all the practical stuff around getting a contract role and setting up on your own – deciding if you can be a sole trader or if you need a company (which isn't as hard as it sounds – honestly!).

One of the biggest steps forward that you've already made is buying this book and reading it! If I had access to this kind of book when I was starting out, it would have been an absolute godsend and would have saved me a load of money and time. I often say to people who come to me seeking advice on moving into contracting "I wish I had met me when I was your age". Without being big-headed or conceited, I firmly believe that there are people around you whom you already know that can help you. Sometimes you just don't know it. I was talking recently to a work colleague (contractor), who had worked with me for 7 months. We were discussing new business opportunities and he just mentioned that he had finished up a website for a friend of his. I leapt on this valuable piece of information. We are now planning to get a new business venture up and running that I had wanted to make happen for some time and all I was short of (apart from time- which is my usual problem!) was a web developer. I'd just never asked him if he had that skill.

The fact that you are reading this book also means that you've asked yourself if there's something better out there. Perhaps you've wanted to be your own boss, run your own life, work from home, have more free time to pursue other hobbies... whatever the reason, you're thinking there's something more for you and you want to change your current situation.

And this is one of the biggest steps forward you can make. It's about reaching out to the future and believing that there is more. I came across a saying recently

"there is nothing more frustrating than those who carry on doing the same things and expect a different outcome"

It is so true – people moan and whine about their current situation but aren't prepared to do anything about it. They almost expect a miracle to occur. I have said to my wife in the past, when she looked longingly at a great big house, "Well, if that's what you want, we'll go and get it but we have to be doing something different to what we're doing now". You have to act to make things change.

I am a firm believer in fate. Things all happen for a reason. If you reach out with a positive mind, with a desire to do something different, things will happen, people will come your way. It's the nature of the universe. There are lots of inspirational books out there on this subject, written by people who are themselves very successful. A major thing they have in common is that they believe that somehow things will come together – sometimes they don't even have a great plan.

Read this:

"Believe that things will work out, follow you intuition and curiosity. Trust your heart even when it leads you off the well-worn path. You have to trust that the dots will somehow connect in your future. The only way to do great work is to love what you do. If you haven't found it yet, keep looking. Don't settle. As with all matters of the heart, you'll know when you find it. Have the courage to follow your heart and

intuition. They somehow already know what you truly want to become. Everything else is secondary."

It's one of the most inspirational pieces of writing I've ever come across. It appeals directly to me and where I'm trying to head. I hope it does something for you too. Any idea who wrote this? You'll never believe it – one of the greatest minds to ever walk on this planet – Steve Jobs, CEO, Apple Inc. Can you believe a mind like that and he thought this way, somehow things just plug together? What it's about is allowing all this to happen. First of all, you have to give permission. In your mind. In your actions.

So you know how it goes - if you never try, you will never know. Equally, there is no point launching yourself into a different life and not knowing what the risks are. It's important to know what you're getting into and working out yourself if you've got what it takes.

The next few sections are focused on just this.

So what is a contractor anyway?

There are many different types of contractor but the majority fit into the following buckets:

- Long term, full time specialist resources, focused on one client (e.g. project management, change management)
- Interim resources, long term, full time, focused on one client, with specific operational responsibilities (e.g. Operations Director, Managing Director)
- Freelancers, Short term specialist resources, focused on many clients (e.g. training course providers, coaching/mentoring services)

The main differences between these are how you manage clients and get work.

Long Term Contract Resource

This is the most typical kind of contracting work and usually takes the form of a client needing someone to work inside their company to perform some specialist role, either because they don't have that skill in-house or because they don't have enough of that kind of resource or not enough good ones with little or no line accountability. Contract duration is usually a minimum of 3 months but clients can offer 6-12 months even at the outset, in order to attract the right kind of contractor. Typically, the work is project based, usually an 'outcome-focused' piece of work – something the client needs to achieve in a given timescale – it has a defined start and a defined end point, sometimes referred to as success criteria.

The range of roles varies enormously from administration/support right through to Programme Director levels. Day Rates are the norm but at the more junior end these can be hourly rates. Some roles come with line management responsibilities and can mean managing permanent resources for more senior positions. Sometimes the client is looking to get some contract resources in for a very short term to allow the permanent resources to learn sufficiently to take over the running of the project or programme, when things have been set up.

Occasionally, clients will bring in contractors and attempt to lure them into permanent employment, which can work well for both parties, allowing them both to see each other in action before making a long-term commitment (perish the thought!).

Interim Management Contract Resource

Interim management is generally a term used where a person is employed specifically because of what they know or because of their specialist skills in order to deliver a set of defined outcomes for a client's business. Examples would be Operations, IT and Finance Director roles, management of big, complex programmes such as Management Buy-Outs (MBO), Initial Public Offerings (IPO), mergers and acquisitions and system implementations. Often, these are senior appointments made on a fixed term contract based on a day rate and they sometimes have a temporary seat on the Board of the company. Interims are often used where recruiting a permanent person is going to take too long and a solution to the resource gap is needed quickly. Typically, the client can be quite desperate to get something delivered like a big change or system/process implementation. Rates in these cases can be quite high, usually because the appointee is going to experience a tough time and long hours etc.

Interims typically have line management and profit and loss responsibility across large teams and they are expected to deliver outcomes or manage the team through a period of significant change but also develop their team whilst they are in the role. They often act as a mentor to not only their direct reports but also into the Board of the company. They bring their wealth of experience to bear on the situation facing them but do not have the political pressures of a permanent employee trying to move up the organisation. Having said that, in a similar way to long term contractors, many interims end up being 'converted' into permanent employees. The client has an opportunity to see how the interim 'fits in' and then makes them an offer they can't refuse – once they've become indispensible that is!

It depends what you're after. If you'd prefer the security of a permanent role, then going interim can be a useful way to get you through the door.

Freelance Contract Resource

Freelance practise varies greatly but this type of work is generally more focused on providing a service or product over a short time frame, sometimes in only a few days. Freelancers are characterised by having many clients, often simultaneously. The term is used more frequently in industries such as journalism, publishing, film making, photography, event management, coaching, training and web design.

While this can be very interesting and motivating, it can result in much lower numbers of days worked in a year. There can be a good deal of uncertainty and irregular income streams. You will often be working on your own or independently as part of a team. But this can be offset by the ability to be able to work from home or work flexibly at times to suit you. People in this type of work can often charge much higher day rates. I've known trainers charge £1,500/day but then only work 2 days a week – it's all about choices! To make this kind of model work, you need to have access to a large network or establish partners and supplier arrangements that provide you with regular assignments.

Comparison of Permanent and Contract Resource

Whichever route you go down, you will be faced with pretty much the same questions and issues addressed in this book. These are all forms of flexible working, a damn site more flexible than a permanent resource can expect. It is worth highlighting the main differences between permanent and contractor roles, just so we're all on the same page.

	Permanent Employee	Contractor, Interim or Freelancer
Pay	Monthly – in response to paid work offered by the employer	Daily, Weekly, Monthly or fixed fee at the end of a contract – for services previously agreed to provided to the employer (client) by your company
Tax	PAYE, National Insurance, low flexibility	PAYE, National Insurance (in some situations, not always), Dividends (at low tax), high flexibility
Hours	Usually fixed	Flexible
Notice	One month to twelve months	Can be a week but usually a month
Holidays	Paid - 20 to 30 days each year	Unpaid, flexible as to how much your cashflow can stand
Redundancy/ Sick Pay/ Maternity/ Paternity Leave/ Pension/ Training & Development	Yes	No
Private Health Care/ Company Car/Social Events	Potentially	No

If you cower at the idea of not having a steady income, fixed hours and paid holidays, then contracting may not be for you. Don't give up just yet though. Read on and let me convince you a little more!

Don't go thinking you have to be an expert or full of grey hair before you can go contracting. It's simply not the case. More and more people are choosing to work this way from an early age. I have known contractors who have gained a degree, joined a contracting company (that specialises in providing graduate resources) and get straight into some really interesting work. It comes down to your attitude and your self-belief. If you think you can do it and you put yourself across successfully to a potential client, the possibilities are endless.

If clients can see themselves working with you and you are enthusiastic and deliver good output consistently, then you can start anywhere – believe me. Your rate may not be brilliant to start with but you have to start somewhere and build up. I recently placed a psychology graduate whom I met while she was working as a waitress. She is really positive and has a fantastic attitude to work and life in general. We worked together to get her CV sorted and figured out what she'd be comfortable doing in a company. She's now a project administrator at a well known high-street bank. It's a start and she loves it! You can start any time, you just have to believe you can.

What is the best way to describe yourself?

It can be difficult to know how to describe yourself when you get into contracting. Sometimes, you're a contractor, sometimes a consultant, a freelancer, an independent, a management consultant. It depends on what you're comfortable with and what fits.

Consultants can probably best be thought of as specialists that are brought into a company to solve a particular problem. They tend to be in a position to offer advice without necessarily the accountability for implementing their recommendations. They may be perceived to have expertise in a particular area. They will often be known to a specific Manager or Director in a company and may have a relationship that goes back years – in fact, in many cases, the Manager or Director has often worked for that consultancy company in the past. Consultants used to have a reputation of spending a long time finding out what the company does, taking all the best ideas from the employees, summarising it in a great big report with plenty of recommendations, getting paid a load of cash for doing this and then clearing off into the distance. The classic comment used to be that all consultants did was take your watch and then tell you the time!

These days, consultants are a lot more accountable. The best ones are prized because of their analytical AND implementation skills. So they take their own recommendations and go forward to make them happen. They still charge a lot of money but companies are now driving down the consultants' day rates and they are becoming more competitive. They have armies of young go-getters who flog themselves to death, working very hard and usually very long hours in order to get up their own promotion ladder. They are reasonably well paid but are typically incentivised via their internal bonus structure.

Contractors are sometimes regarded as lower class citizens compared to consultants. Contractors are brought in for their specific skill set to solve a problem in the same way as consultants but the focus is much more on implementation not just advice. Clients will have less come back on a contractor if things go wrong. I have known big consulting firms lose tens of thousands of pounds and occasionally millions of pounds in fees when they don't deliver. It would be very unusual for a contractor to face the same fate. And there are insurances (Personal Indemnity Insurance - PII) that can be taken out to limit the financial effects of this. You can often get a mix of consultants and contractors working on projects side by side.

Remember that although these consultants often have a great brand behind them, often have amazing qualifications and experience and are keen as mustard, they might actually be earning less than you as a contractor!

The way in which you describe yourself can often be dictated by the industry you work in. As mentioned above, freelancers is a term used more in media and creative industries. My advice when starting out is to refer to yourself as an independent contractor or just as a contractor. If you are quite senior and have the relevant experience, you could refer to yourself as an independent management consultant (that is how I describe myself).

Going forward in the rest of the book, I will use the term contractor to cover all these different types of flexible working.

Clients v Customers

It is important that you get to use the right term to describe the people that you work for as a contractor. They are your 'boss' but not in the same way as for permanent employees. They are your customer in terms of your business but I would always use the term 'client' when referring to the company I'm working with. This is an industry term, borne out of consultancy. The term is borne out of the Latin word *cliens* which means "dependent" or "follower", which stresses the difference in the bond of the relationship formed. The distinction is sometimes drawn by saying that a customer is someone who you do business with once, whereas a client is someone you're doing business with and develop a business relationship with them to such an extent that they want to continue doing business with you. You and your client build up trust so that they will often come to you for advice over time.

Where are you trying to get to?

I always ask this question of people who ask me about contracting. It's important to get a grasp of what each person is about. It's truly amazing what comes out and I've learned never to judge a book by its cover. The trick is working out what the route is to get there. I've come across a lot of people who are very intent on their future, clear about the end game (where they'd like to end up) but not the foggiest clue about how they're going to get there. And when it comes to it, when you do present them with the route, they run off into the distance realising how much hard work it's going to be.

There is no one route to achieving your goals - you have to try many different routes and often several routes in parallel. Some will work, others will not. It's about how you bounce back and keep going after experiencing failures that counts.

So you need to think about what success looks like for you. It might be that you want to work for a number of years and pack it all in and retire early. In which case, you are going to need to know how much is enough for you to do that. It might be you want to work 9 months of the year and take 3 months off, or work a contract and take a few weeks out. Or like me, go hell for leather to do as many days as you can because you have expensive outgoings! – including house, children, school fees, nice holidays etc.

You can do this yourself easily. I like the simple method outlined by www.mindtools.com. (click on Toolkit, Time Management and Personal Goal Setting). There's lots of useful stuff on this website about goal setting.

In summary, you think about the big picture, your long term goals, then break them down to shorter and shorter periods of time until you end up with a pretty granular 'to do' list. But this is important so that you understand what is important to you and where becoming a contractor fits into the grand scheme for you personally. It can help you prioritise and work out how to ensure you achieve a balance that works for you (see the next section).

Assuming you're still reading and you haven't decided that you'd rather be a monk, then a key think to know at this early stage is that, financially, contracting is going to keep you afloat – or put another way "to keep you in the manner to which you want to become accustomed!" Below is a table that roughly calculates the day rate you need to earn to match an equivalent 'permanent' salary.

Permanent Employee Salary	Equivalent Contractor Daily Rate
£20,000	£99
£30,000	£140
£40,000	£180
£50,000	£216
£60,000	£252
£70,000	£303
£80,000	£341
£90,000	£399
£100,000	£437
£125,000	£537
£150,000	£672
£175,000	£771
£200,000	£869
£250,000	£1,118

These figures assume that you are outside of what is called IR35 (basically a tax that was introduced to stop permanent employees setting their own limited companies, working for the same company and paying a lot less tax – it used to happen a lot in the IT industry) and that you have a standard tax allowance.

For those of you who want to know how this is worked out, the details are included in the Appendices.

This table should at least answer a fundamental question, which is, how much do I have to earn as a contractor in order to bring in as much as I did on my permanent role? You then need to work out how much a typical contractor is likely to earn in your given field of work. If these figures don't stack up for you, then I suggest you close the book and don't think about contracting again or more positively, think about how you might improve your skills or experience to get to a place where the figures do stack.

Achieving a Balance that works for you

When you're getting started, the type of contracting you do is driven by some key decisions that only you can make. It's all about choices as I said before but it's also about achieving a balance that works for you. There are 4 key drivers to balance.

1. The amount of money you earn – your rate
2. The amount of pressure/stress you can handle
3. The amount of time you are prepared to spend away from home
4. The amount of change you can take – the frequency of moving between contracts

I know hundreds of contractors. The majority go into contracting to earn more money than they could hope to do in a full time job. But they also are comfortable with the idea of moving on from one place to another – they embrace changes of scene rather than seeing them as a barrier. This is something that you do get to appreciate over time. The thrill of the chase. Quite a lot of them – me included – spend more time away from home than a lot of people do. The extreme is 5 days away from home each week, leaving Monday morning, coming back Friday night. For some people, this would be unacceptable but as you go further and further into contracting, the company that you're working for is going to expect more and more from you, often expecting you to be on site every working day. So there is a balance that you need to achieve between the amount you earn, time away from home and the amount of change you can take.

So let's look at this balance.

1. **Rate of pay** – this depends on your role, your experience and the size of company (client). As an administrator, you are most likely to start out on an hourly rate in a job. This will earn you anywhere between £8/hr - £20/hr (£65/day - £160/day). Sometimes you can get paid overtime.

   As a junior project manager, with experience in a permanent role, you could expect to get £300/day upwards, depending on the size of the project, the complexity of the role and the level of responsibility you would be expected to take on.

   As a programme manager, it really does depend – these can range from £500/day to over £1000/day, again depending on size, complexity and level, as mentioned above. Finally, for Programme Directors, these are bespoke roles and can command anywhere between £800/day to over £2,000/day. But at this point, you are in a very niche environment. You're also getting into full blown Top 5 Major Consulting firm territory. These guys are under pressure and are being forced to reduce their prices in order to keep revenue coming in and not having expensive people sitting around "on the bench" – i.e. not earning anything for the firm. So their bottom rates for analysts are coming in at around £600/day and even fairly Senior Managers are being charged in at around £1,000/day, which makes for a very keenly priced market if clients can pick contractors or a Big 5 consultant for a similar price. We will return to our Big 5 friends later.

   I've pulled together some research from all the roles that have arrived in my inbox. It highlights the main roles that get offered by agencies and the rates that they are offering.

Job Role	Lowest Rate	Highest Rate	Average Rate
All	£250	£1,000	£565
Interim	£500	£1,000	£737
Programme Mgr	£450	£1,000	£677
Change Mgr	£400	£800	£539
Project Mgr	£250	£900	£537
Finance Mgr	£400	£650	£510
Business Analyst	£400	£550	£480
Test Mgr	£350	£600	£460
PMO Mgr	£325	£550	£445

In this survey, Interim roles command the highest day rates, 30% higher than the average contractor rate and 10% higher than Programme Manager/Director positions. A bit of an anomaly is the Business Analyst role. I would normally expect this to be equivalent to or slightly higher than the PMO Manager role in terms of rate, but it just goes to show that there is healthy demand for BAs.

So hopefully this is a useful guide for you to work out broadly where your rate is likely to be. The reality is that it will be dependent on a number of factors including the time of year that you apply for a role and your own particular circumstances (i.e. who you know), the general condition of the market and other factors. Check with agents and look on-line for roles.

2. **Amount of Pressure/Stress** – this is generally directly linked to the amount you're earning. Big stress and big pressure usually

comes with high day rates. The higher up you operate, the bigger the expectations from you, the more demanding a client can be, which leads directly to increased pressure on you and potentially increased stress in your life. If you're gunning for the higher rate, you must absolutely expect the client to want to get the most out of you. Expect long hours, expect constant decision making, expect to have to really know your stuff and be constantly directing people, expect a team that needs your input constantly. This need not be a problem. You could decide to take a contract role that is well within your capability. So be a project manager when you know you could be a programme manager.

The level of pressure and stress can come from the type of contractor you choose to be. On longer term projects (6 months and beyond), you have a chance to settle in and some days are better than others. If you're doing short term work (like training), you're more likely to feel more regular stress/pressure peaks and troughs as you scrabble to deliver what the client wants in a very short space of time.

So you need to ask yourself what level of stress and pressure you can and want to handle and position this against the day rate you think you can achieve or need.

3. **Time away from home** – in my experience, this doesn't vary too much. Generally, the kind of job most people get into is project work – not always but in most cases. This means a set of activities with a defined start and end point, a fixed budget and some fairly major outcomes expected. So, there's time pressure and people are expected to be working on the project full-time. In most cases, this involves being on site 5 days a week, but more and more we're seeing companies that insist that their employees take time to work

at home and this can extend to contractors. Friday's are often a classic for "working from home". Or there are examples of people having to take a day in the week at home – sometimes because there isn't enough space in the office for them if they all turn up!

So, being relatively close to your client site is going to be a bonus and give you flexibility to get home and be on client site as the client expects. Where this starts to fall apart is when the client isn't nearby or you live in a non-central part of the country. A typical rule of thumb is if you have to travel more than 90 minutes to your client site, then you probably need to think about working away from home for some nights of the week. The reason for this is down to expectation. As a contractor, the client needs to feel as though they are getting their pound of flesh for the rate they are paying. Sure, they've got themselves into a position where they don't have enough of the right kind of people to do what they want to do, but it still sticks in their throat that they have to pay someone even quite junior £80k/yr, which is often more than a lot of people are getting in their company. This translates into putting in an extra bit of effort and not leaving bang on the dot at 5.30pm. Or arriving early is another contractor favourite – sending emails at 7am, when it's quiet and no-one's around can be a real client sweetener. This can creep up on you and before you know it, you're leaving work late, getting back home late, to find everyone in bed and then you're up early the next morning and you're wondering "What the hell am I doing!" You get tired, your work fails and you get into a bit of a death spiral. The answer is to balance time at home and time at work. Staying away some evening's can just take the pressure off a little. Having said that I know people who will travel up to 2 ½ hours per day each way, just so they can go home each night.

They counter leaving on the dot by saying they can work on the train, and this can work for some clients but not all.

The table below is taken from a survey of a number of roles that have appeared in my inbox over a period of time, the same set of data as for the rates by role in the previous section.

Location	Lowest Rate	Highest Rate	Average Rate
All	£525	£1,000	£565
London	£400	£1,000	£600
NW	£450	£800	£590
Midlands	£300	£1000	£515
SW	£350	£650	£510
Scotland	£380	£700	£505
SE	£250	£750	£480
Yorkshire	£325	£800	£480

Not surprisingly, London offers the highest average rate, commanding up to 25% more than those in the lowest paid regions. Also, in this survey, London offers as many as 4 times the number of roles for contractors.

If you are not prepared to travel, and you live remotely, then you expect fewer contracts and lower rates. Whether you love it or hate it, London has the best rates – "a man who is tired of London is tired of life", so the saying goes, but if you are within striking distance of London, that is a great start.

Other major conurbations are ok, but there is a lot less regular work around. In my experience, Birmingham, Manchester, Bristol,

Leeds, Edinburgh and Glasgow are the next best in terms of available contracts. But it can be very much industry dependent.

I live in Oxfordshire. I work in London. I bought a place in London a few years ago just because I knew I was going to spend a lot of time there and you do get to a point where you get fed up with living out of a suitcase. I work away 5 days a week, but have done for over 15 years, as a consultant with some of the big firms and then independently. It does create difficulties but as you rise up the contracting ladder, as I have done, then the client expects more and more. I have had years of working till gone 9pm every weekday and being full on during the day and I just couldn't contemplate the idea of travelling 2 hours each way home, no matter how much I love my family. I would be 6 feet under.

Your home situation is a big determining factor in where you strike this balance. If you're on your own, then you can do what you like. If you have a draw back to your home – strong friendship ties or animals (cats, dogs, horses..) then you have to take this into account.

It gets trickier when you're considering your partner and your children. Before getting too far into making a move into contracting, you need to talk through with your other half about what balance you all need to achieve. If you have very active children who are out doing sports or after school activities and your other half doesn't drive in the dark, then that clearly places a constraint on what you can do. If you have a very strong partner, it may be possible to be away from home more often. The important thing is that you talk about it and come to an agreement about what will work best – in an ideal world. I say this because, rest assured, your first contract will probably fall outside the boundaries you've just set for yourself and you then have to make decisions about if you can make it work. You all have to realise that the boundaries of "what's ideal" will need to flex and change over time. But if it causes problems in your relationship, you need to re-think and re-balance. In the extreme, contracting can be quite a selfish thing to do. If you're in my position, you leave home each week with the sole intention of working your socks off for the client, doing a great job and then, on a Friday, you return home. My wife is incredibly strong, our children both incredibly active. But my wife's philosophy on this is "The client gets you during the week and that's fine, as long as I get you all weekend". And that's been the deal for the last 15 years. And, I've only broken that rule twice, having negotiated more time off than I worked at the weekend – an extra day - and an agreement to take Mrs G. out for a slap up dinner paid for by the client!

4. **Amount of Change** – the other key factor is the amount of change you can cope with whilst you're contracting. This is driven largely by the type of contracting work you decide to get into. If you choose project work, then you may be on 3-6 month contracts or longer, in which case the level of change between contracts is fairly low. You can get into a routine, much like you have in a permanent role. At the other end of the spectrum is training type work or short term consulting work like coaching. In this type of work, you will be changing clients constantly and doing short bursts of work with them and you have to constantly find new opportunities and leads.

So contracting is all about achieving BALANCE

This is a balance between how much you want to earn, what level you want to operate at, where you work and how much you want to be at home and the level of change you can cope with. Only you can work out what is most important to you given your own circumstances. Talk to your family, talk to your friends, talk to your business acquaintances and work out the balance that is going to be best for you.

What is my income likely to be?

It's important to know what you're likely to receive as an income by being a contractor. The basics are you earn income from your day rate, you choose how many days you work per year. As you do this, you will incur costs like travel and accommodation, so that's an expense that comes off the rate you earn. After all your costs come off, the Government will then tax you and the amount depends on what kind of business you have set up. Broadly speaking, the two main options are setting up a Limited Company or being what's called a sole trader. Once the tax has been paid, then what is left is yours to give to yourself.

Let's take an example for a Limited Company. There are broadly three simple steps:

1. Income (a) – Costs (b) = Gross Profit (c)
2. Gross Profit (c) – Corporation Tax (d) = Net Profit (e)
3. Net Profit (e) – Taxes (f) = Net Payment into your bank (g)

1.	**Gross Profit**	
(a)	Income (Rate – assumed £500/day, Number of days worked/yr – 200 days (5-6 weeks for holiday))	£100,000
(b)	Total Costs*	£23,172
(c)	Gross Profit	£76,828
2.	**Net Profit**	
(d)	Corporation Tax (gross profit x 20%)	£15,366
(e)	Net Profit (amount that can be distributed as dividends – see later)	£61,462
3.	**Net Payment into your Bank**	
(f)	Total Taxes and NI payable	£7,770
	Net Income (net profit + salary – taxes)	£61,384
(g)	Monthly Net Payment into your Bank	**£5,115**

* Breakdown of Total Costs			
Salary (you pay yourself the minimum amount to avoid paying NI)		£7,692	
Expenses (assuming your expenses are not paid by the client)		£15,480	
- Accommodation (assuming worst case 4 nights away from home per week, 34 weeks (160 nights) @ £60/night)	£8,100		
- Travel (assuming train travel, once per week: £50/week)	£1,700		
- Taxis/Other travel: £20/week	£680		
- Meals/Expenses: £20/day	£3,400		
- Phone Bill: £50/month	£600		
- Other Costs	£1,000		

The reason for hitting you with this at this stage in the book (without too much explanation about limited companies, corporation tax and dividends) is that you might take one look at this and think that it just isn't worth it for you. On the other hand, it might just start to make you think that this IS the way forward for you. Now some of the assumptions may not be relevant for you, so you can start to play around with the figures and if taxis and accommodation can be wiped out, you could easily add a further £10,000 to your gross profit.

Now, if we were to do the same example for a Sole Trader, the example would look like this:

1. Income (a) – Costs (b) = Gross Profit (c)

2. Gross Profit (c) – Tax allowance = Taxable Income (d)

3. Taxable Income (d) – Taxes (e) = Net Payment into your bank (f)

1. **Gross Profit**	
(a) Income (Rate: assumed £500/day, Number of days worked/yr: 200 days (5-6 weeks for holiday))	£100,000
(b) Total Costs (as above but not inc salary, you get taxed on the full amount of your earnings, less expenses only)	£15,480
(c) Gross Profit	£84,520
2. **Taxable Income**	
(d) Taxable Income (gross profit less personal allowance)	£75,080
3. **Net Payment into your Bank**	
(e) Total Taxes and NI payable	£27,664
Net Income (net profit + salary – taxes)	£56,856
(f) Monthly Net Payment into your Bank	**£4,738**

If you go to the website – www.breakfreegocontracting.com – under the Resources tab, you can put in your own parameters and work out your net monthly payment for your own situation.

I know it's a lot to take in at this stage, but it's important you get some basics about how the different structures work and how much of your hard earned pennies go straight to the tax man! And you can do a straight comparison and work out with your personal circumstances, which option is best for you. As you can see, there isn't a massive difference between the options.

ARE YOU CUT OUT FOR CONTRACTING?

It is really quite crucial that you understand who you are, what your strengths and your weaknesses are. To get along in the contract world, you need to have get up and go, get on with just about everyone, not be a quitter, not be someone who loses their temper, be able to put up with uncertainty, be a networker, be healthy, be reliable, be a hard worker, be good at what you do, be able to deliver good outputs on time and to good quality.

What does it take to be a successful contractor?

Below is a list of what it takes to be a successful contractor. It's not exhaustive but it's a list of the top 10 things you need for contracting to work. If you can honestly answer yes to at least 8 out of 10 of these characteristics, you have a chance. You will still need to work on the other two in order to be really successful.

10 characteristics of a successful contractor
1. Able to cope with risk and uncertainty
2. Flexible in approach to work – can deal with ambiguity
3. Able to fit in, get on with almost everyone, work well as part of a team and please the client
4. Happy to work sufficient hours – often unsociable – to get the job done
5. Level headed, not given to outbursts or extreme reactions
6. Able to communicate objectives, work required and deliverables, simply and clearly
7. Able to deliver excellent, quality outcomes, on time and repeatedly
8. Exudes confidence in their own ability to deliver
9. Not precious about hierarchy or position as long as the job gets done
10. Organised

I'm going to briefly explain each one of these characteristics because it's so important you understand the criteria before you enter the game of contracting.

1. Able to cope with risk and uncertainty –
    This is an absolute must and is why it's #1 on the list. There are risks in contracting. You have to be able to cope with:
    a. Potentially irregular income
        Gone are the days when you got a regular payslip arriving in the post or your inbox. Can you honestly look yourself in the mirror and say "I can cope with this"? Can you think about not necessarily being able to consistently plan to pay the mortgage, the school fees, your loans? Or can you pull

together a financial plan that allows you to cope for a number of months. Do you have the drive to succeed and get work consistently to bring in significantly more money than you were earning in a permanent role? Can you see yourself doing that, time after time, year after year? If you can, move on.

b. Stops and starts in contracts

Gone are the days when your boss pulled you into the office and told you where you were going next. It's going to be up to you. Can you cope with moving on from one contract to another, coping with the disruption to your personal life and your arrangements and the relationships you so carefully built with the client? Can you see yourself constantly being ready for a new challenge, starting afresh potentially every few months? If you can, you're doing great, move on.

c. Disruptions to contracts

You'll be living in an uncertain world, where you're gut instinct gets more acute. It's a life where things can change all around you and you've got to be able to cope with it and not panic. You land a contract, then suddenly something changes and you're out. No fault of your own, just damn bad luck sometimes. Can you see yourself picking yourself up off the floor and cracking on into another contract? If you can, even better, move on!

d. Potentially not being able to find work when you need it

The fur-lined rut isn't there to protect you while you find your next role and cosset you while you're waiting around.

Contracting is all about timing – being in the right place at the right time for the right opportunity. Most times it works – with careful planning that we will come to later – but sometimes, it just doesn't. Can you cope with the situation where you are burning through your cash, you wake up each day and have no job to go to and there appears to be nothing coming up over the horizon. Are you going to curl up in a ball and quit? Or can you deal with this and never, ever stop believing in yourself? Believing that, by persevering, you will get another role and it will come your way because you will make it happen? If you can, you're almost there, keep going!

e. Motivating yourself and being disciplined

Remember the days when you just turned up at work and didn't really give a damn, just wafted your way through the day and delivered nothing? All gone. As a contractor, you are on show all the time, you are constantly being assessed by the client who is working out if they are getting value for money because they know they can get a replacement if they need to. Do you have the strength to be able to motivate yourself daily, to go the extra mile, to constantly watch yourself, motivate yourself and choose your attitude positively? Is this you?

f. Being out of the loop

Yes, a fair bit of the time, you are out there on your own, making your own decisions, your own way forward, you're deciding which course of action to take, which contract to go for, which person to trust. You have to be able to cope with this and be confident in your own abilities.

If all this sends shivers down your spine, stop reading, shut the book, make a cup of tea and get settled back down into your fur lined rut. There's nothing wrong with that, it's just that contracting is probably not for you, or it may not be the right timing for you yet. I've taken the time to really go to town on this first question because I believe it is so important. It's what fundamentally defines if you're going to be able to make it past the first step. The others are important but this one is about your character and your inner beliefs.

2. Flexible in approach to work - can deal with ambiguity.

    You might think that when clients want contractors, they have everything sorted – job spec, deliverables, clear view of what they need to be successful. Well, in general, they don't. So you need to be able to arrive on client site and start working from Day 1 with a potentially quite vague idea about what is going on. You may be the person who has to define clearly what it is you need to do and agree this with the client.

3. Able to fit in, get on with almost everyone, work well as part of a team and please the client.

    You need to be able to arrive at a new workplace and instantly be able to get on with most people around you. If you don't, you will get found out very quickly and the client will be having words with you. This is not to say you have to be a wall flower and never challenge people, it's just that you need to be tactful early on.

    Be clear about who the client is – who is signing off your invoices or your timesheets. These are the people to please. Be absolutely sure they know who you are and what you are doing for them.

4. Happy to work sufficient hours – often unsocial – to get the job done

    The client will not expect you to be a strict 9 to 5-er. They will expect you to work the hours required to get the job done. This can mean working late on some, most or even every day, depending on what you've been asked to do. It can mean working at home and working at weekends. You will have to be prepared to do this. If there is a reason you can't work longer than normal office hours, again, contracting is probably not for you.

5. Level headed, not given to outbursts or extreme reactions

    This is crucial especially at the start of contract. As you gain more experience, you will be able to suss out a place in the first week. You will find lots of things wrong. It may be completely at odds with your experience to date and may make your blood boil. But you cannot let this spill out to your team or your client. It's best to write down your observations after the first week – you won't be far wrong.

6. Able to communicate objectives, work required and deliverables, simply and clearly

    A key ability is to be able to communicate concisely, with your team and with your client. The best way is to write down objectives and deliverables required and ensure the client agrees and that the rest of your team understands what it is you are meant to be doing.

7. Able to deliver excellent, quality outcomes, on time and repeatedly

    You have to be able to know what good looks like. It doesn't have to be better than what the client has experienced to date, but it does help. If you can take an idea that the client has and basically improve it, you will do well. Most clients will expect you to deliver a good output on time, even if it means you have to put in significant hours to get it delivered. Eventually, they will cut you some slack.

8. Exudes confidence in their own ability to deliver

    The last thing a client wants is someone who is forever asking for guidance. You have to have a confident attitude about you to take ownership. "Give me something and I'll deliver it for you." That's what clients want – someone they can trust, someone who is going to make them look good.

9. Not precious about hierarchy or position as long as the job gets done

    Contracting is definitely not about position or hierarchy – it's about getting a job done. It is important that you get the right job title for your contract but your deliverables should do the talking.

10. Organised

    It sounds obvious but if you are a generally untidy person or are not very good at managing your time or getting to meetings on time, then this will soon grate on a client. If this is a problem for you, it's surmountable – sort it.

If after reading this, you think you can score more than 8, potentially by changing some of your habits, then contracting could be a route for you. Let's move on to some other checks you can make.

Your Personal Profile

I often advise people to take some simple personality tests so that they can understand where there true strengths and weaknesses are. It's about what makes you tick and you understanding that, possibly for the first time in your life. It's about understanding what your values are and how that will translate into a client world.

There are many personality profile tests that you can take. The value of taking one or more of these is to understand more about yourself, about what drives you and how you compare with other people around you. A simple test you can complete is called the Myers-Briggs test, leading you to a Myers-Briggs Type Indicator (MBTI). Essentially, the test measures you against four different dimensions

Dimension (sometimes called Dichotomies)	
Extraversion (E)	Introversion (I)
Sensing (S)	Intuition (N)
Thinking (T)	Feeling (F)
Judging (J)	Perception (P)

You complete a questionnaire and depending on how you answer the questions, you are assigned one of sixteen possible profile types.

This test has been evolved over decades and has been taken by hundreds of thousands of people, if not millions. So, it is statistically significant. It's not without its critics, but as a first pass, it's a useful step for you as a potential contractor to measure yourself against the possible profiles to see if you're close to the typical profile of a contractor or not.

For a contractor/consultant, the most common profiles are ENFJ, ENTP, ENTJ, ESTJ (most prolific), ESFJ and ESTP.

This is not to say that if you are an Introvert by the measure of this test that you cannot be a contractor, it's just that you don't have a typical profile of contractors as measured by this test.

A very good website that allows you to do the test free of charge and tells you your profile type and provides lots of additional information can be found at www.humanmetrics.com.

Click on Jung Typology Test and you can take the test.

You can try other personality tests at www.similarminds.com.

With all of these tests, just remember, it's giving you an indication of your personality. Don't get too hung up on it!

Your Personal Risk Profile

It is also useful to understand your attitude to risk. I was once asked by an independent financial advisor what I thought my attitude to risk was. I said, I thought I was fairly middle of the road. He told me I was 'off the scale'!

Again, there is no right or wrong answer in this area but taking a test can give you an interesting and independent perspective on your risk profile. There are many tests around but I would recommend one to be found on www.humanmetrics.com . They have a test called the Risk Attitudes Profiler. Just 22 questions but it does give you an insight which can be very useful to you as you understand more about yourself and make the decision to move into contracting or not. This test costs less than £3.00 but is worthwhile.

If you prefer to take a free risk profiling test, try Psychtests Risk-Taking Test. You can find this at www.testyourself.psychtests.com. Click on the Lifestyle and Attitudes tab and select the Risk-Taking Test.

Your SAVE analysis

Understanding what skills, attitudes, values and experience you bring to the client is crucial. I get people to write these down in a simple 4 box diagram.

Skills	Attitude
(what is your primary set of skills that a client would value?) e.g. Project Management Relationship Management Selling Negotiating Change Management	(what would you say are the words to describe your behaviours?) e.g. Hard Working Reliable Credible
Values	Experience
(what are your key beliefs about what is important to you and in business?) e.g. Integrity Honesty Fairness	(what are the main areas of activity where you have gained knowledge?) e.g. Managing Projects Managing and Directing teams Large scale contract negotiation

It can be useful to run this by a few friends and see what they would put in the boxes to describe you. It can be quite an eye opener to have a view from others. In some cases, your perception of yourself can be quite different from how others perceive you. So, get them to be honest. It will help you.

Once you understand these, together with your personal profile, you can get a handle on what it is you're offering the client. Use the words you and others have written about you in your CV. Use these words when you are describing yourself to an agent. Get used to using these words about yourself. It's about you understanding how you tick and what it is that you offer.

This isn't a one shot pass either. As you go forward in the contracting world, you will change, you will get more experience and your SAVE will change with you. So remember to keep it up to date.

Your SWOT analysis

This is about understanding your own Strengths, Weaknesses, Opportunities and Threats (SWOT). You may have come across this in a business setting to describe and evaluate new projects or ventures but it is equally valid in a personal setting. It's about specifying an objective and identifying the internal and external factors that are favourable and unfavourable to achieving that objective.

In this case your objective is 'to become a successful contractor'.

Again, this can be thought of as a two by two matrix.

	Helpful to achieving your objective	Harmful to achieving your objective
Internal Factors	**Strengths** *(what are your characteristics that give you an advantage over other contractors?)* e.g. pragmatic approach, committed, direct relevant experience, stakeholder management and communication skills, negotiation skills, programme delivery capability.	**Weaknesses** *(what are your characteristics that place you at a disadvantage to other contractors?)* e.g. insufficient experience, not used to dealing with Senior Managers, lack of contracting experience, not having managed large enough or complex projects.
External Factors	**Opportunities** *(what are the elements in the contracting world that could create benefits for you ?)* e.g. potential to learn more, gain more experience, earn more money, enjoy life more, be more in control of your own destiny, take more time to do other things, get a better home/work balance	**Threats** *(what are the elements in the contracting world that could cause trouble for you?)* e.g. lack of understanding of contracting, managing difficult situations and /or clients, managing risk of contracting, ensuring family are supportive, management of work/home life balance

Again, it is useful to have others look over your SWOT when you have completed it. They may see things in a different light to you. They may see that you have skills and strengths that are better than you yourself think. They may also see other threats that you would prefer not to think about!

Use this matrix when describing yourself and when constructing your CV. You should of course focus on the positive aspects – your strengths and opportunities. But be aware of your weaknesses. A classic interview question is to ask "so what do you consider are your areas of weakness?" (or more correctly these days, areas for improvement!). Be ready and have an answer to "and what are you doing about it?" Or turn it into a positive – "My weakness is that I'm just too eager to please!"

Your Personal Brand

By completing the SAVE and SWOT analyses above, you should be starting to have a clearer idea about where your key skill sets lie and what you are able to offer clients. Thinking about your own brand is key for you to sort out as you move into contracting. This isn't much more than thinking through how it is that you are going to market yourself. What title are you going to use to describe yourself? It is worth putting some thought into because people will pigeon hole you. You need to be clear with yourself, with agents and with clients about what services you are offering.

It's best to stick to mainstream titles for yourself such as Project Manager, Change Manager, Risk Manager, Programme Director. This means that agents can quickly narrow down what you are and push specific and relevant opportunities your way.

If in your full time job you were a Management Information Controller for example, not many jobs are going to come up with that as a specific title. So you need to look at what skills you do have and figure out the best title for yourself. In the example above, if you're trained as an Accountant, you might brand yourself as an Accountant. This will give you access to clients who need Accountancy services probably most likely on an interim basis.

But if you had managed projects as part of your MI Controller role, you might brand yourself as a Project Finance Manager or Project Controller. This opens up a wide range of opportunities – after all, every large firm runs projects and they need their finances controlled and managed. So thinking about your brand is important because it will maximise your chances of getting a role.

And don't confine yourself to one brand – you can market yourself in different ways to different people. Some clients may want a Change Manager and you may have the skills to do that because you've spent many years running teams or projects and dealt with change throughout that time. Branding yourself in different ways is not a problem, you just need to be careful that you don't come across as a jack of all trades to agents. You will probably need multiple versions of your CV to back up the difference in your branding, and there's more of that in the next section.

A word of caution though. I know lots of people who want to move into contract roles and brand themselves as a project manager. This can be tricky. If you've run lots of projects in your permanent role and they've been successful – i.e. delivered the outcomes on time and on budget – then this can be a route for you. But there are lots of project managers already out there in the contract market place and they are mostly pretty good and most of them will be qualified with at least PRINCE2, which is the main qualification to have in the project management world. You have to work out where your niche is and describe yourself much more specifically to narrow down the field. So there is a balance to be achieved in your branding between being too broad, but very likely to attract clients and being too narrow so that you get no real opportunities coming your way.

Another piece of advice is not necessarily to carry your current job level into contracting. So if you are currently a programme manager, don't necessarily expect that you enter the contracting market at that level. I generally advise people to go one level down (so if you're a programme manager, enter the market as a senior project manager). The reason for this is that clients like to feel as thought they are getting a good deal – a programme manager for project manager money in effect.

Depending on the skills you have, you may achieve more success in interim roles rather than contracting roles. As a reminder, interim roles are more like semi-permanent roles and often do convert into permanent roles. These are typically more senior roles like Finance Manager or Operations Directors for example. So remember to keep this option open, brand yourself accordingly and have a CV specifically made up to appeal to clients who are looking for interims.

Your CV

There are many books and courses and plenty of advice on the internet about how to create a great CV. I have done dozens for people over the years. I am going to give you a quick guide to how you can create a great CV in this section but if you have a tried and trusted method yourself, please move on to the next chapter.

You may not think that this is too important as you may have never really paid much attention to your CV in the past. Your CV is your shop window, your brochure, your advertisement, your promotion, your branding, your marketing. It's the only thing the client looks at when deciding whether to interview you or not. So it is imperative that you give yourself the best possible chance of creating a favourable impression as soon as the client picks up your CV.

There are 6 basic sections to a CV.

1. Personal Details
2. Executive summary
3. Career History
4. Major Work Completed
5. Interests/Hobbies
6. References

1. Personal Details

This section should have your name, address, and contact details. Use your own email address and personal phone number. Avoid any contact details associated with your current employment. You don't have to put on your date of birth. Since the introduction of the Employment Equality (Age) Regulations 2006, age discrimination is now illegal in the recruitment process. Most CVs will have information on them about when you attended school or university, so it doesn't take much to work out roughly how old you are anyway. It's a similar situation for marital status. You don't have to put this on your CV but you might decide it's a positive thing to highlight, and, if so, then do include your marital status. You don't have to include your nationality either, apart from some Government positions, where it is needed. If the job you're applying for includes a fair bit of driving, then you might want to highlight your clean driving licence (i.e. no points), if you have one!

2. Executive Summary

This is the most important section on your CV and lots of CVs don't actually have one. This is a paragraph that describes you and what you are all about. When a potential client picks up your CV, this is the section they will home in on and read. They may not have time to read the rest in detail. Get this section right and you have a fair chance of getting onto the 'call for interview' pile.

This section should start off by informing the reader what you are. "Neil is a [insert a few words describing your key attributes] *Programme Manager* who..."

This is important because what the client wants to see in this section is that you describe your role title (your brand – see above) exactly as the role title that they're looking for. What this also means is that you can and should have multiple versions of your CV that are tailored to specific roles that you might apply for.

So that's the first line of this section! The remainder should bring out what really drives you and get's you out of bed in the morning. Here's what's on my CV right now:

A high influencing, pragmatic Programme Manager with 12 years experience in consulting firms and 5 years senior management experience within Blue Chip companies. A professional change manager who thrives under pressure and who leads, manages and implements change using a well-honed combination of people and project management skills. PRINCE 2 qualified with 15+ year's experience of directing complex change programmes across many countries, across diverse business divisions and across different industry sectors. Strong management and decision-making skills complemented by excellent communication, organisational and presentation skills.

The key things I'm trying to get across to my potential clients is that my key style is as an influencer – I can get people to do things for me, and hence the client, in a nice way. I'm also pragmatic. Clients often want someone who can be flexible in their approach and not 'stick to the book'. These first few words are crucial and they change as you get more experience. Take your cues from the job description that you get for a role. If they want 'systematic' put 'I am systematic...' somewhere in this section! You're just playing back to them what they want to hear. It helps if you really are 'systematic' of course and the rest of your CV should justify it.

The remainder of my executive summary moves on to talk about what the client can expect from me. So I'm pulling out that I combine an approach that is change management based, i.e. people, processes and systems all in one package. I've got the experience (PRINCE 2), I work in complex change arenas and I've worked across many different industries so I'm bringing a wealth of different approaches to this role.

Take time to work on your Executive Summary. You may not get it right first time. Take feedback on it from others around you who know you. Take feedback from agencies that see your CV. Don't be over protective, after all, it's increasing your chances of getting a role.

3. Career History

This is relatively straight forward. This should describe the key roles you've had since leaving school or university. Choose how you format this, but an extract from my CV is shown below. For each role, I put the name of the company and the title of the position I held in bold. Then it's possible for a client to quickly look down a list of roles I've held. The key thing is to keep things succinct – try not to have more than 2 lines of text against each role. This forces you to think very clearly about what the key part of your role was and what *you personally* were responsible for.

CAREER HISTORY

Rapid Effects Ltd., Director

May 2003 – present

Founder of a consultancy firm providing many service lines including project, programme and change management, post merger integration and strategy development/implementation advice to clients across a broad range of industries

4.   Major Work Completed

While the section on Career History summarises into a few words what your role was about, this section should expand on the really key things that you delivered. So if you managed a project, you get a chance to explain what you delivered and what the benefits were. Don't just put down a list of responsibilities. If you do explain your responsibilities, make sure it's brief and describe things that you delivered and can substantiate at an interview. Ideally, you should try to match what you put in here to the job you're applying for. And do bring out some key facts and figures. "Delivered 30% improvement in....", "saved £40m of...", "improved lead-time by 50%". These are tangible things that the potential interviewer will potentially find interesting and relevant to them. They want to know if you've done something similar to what they're trying to do.

5. Interests/Hobbies

Keep this section brief and focus on those interests and hobbies where you can show you've achieved something. Equally, add in those interests where you have a passion and be prepared to talk about this – it can add serious value to an interview, especially if you can strike up an empathy with the interviewer and they can often use it as an ice-breaker.

6. References

References are just details of a couple of people that a prospective client can go and talk to about you and what kind of person you are. I tend to have one who is a friend and can supply a character reference and the other is someone who knows me professionally in my workplace. It's ok to put that 'references can be supplied upon request'. Then, at least you know if the client is interested in you if they ask for these details.

Some top tips about your CV are to keep it up to date, constantly review it, hone it, look at others and plagiarise with pride. It's an important document. If you see one that grabs your attention or the format looks good, don't be afraid to try it out with our own details.

Do have multiple versions of your CV ready for the key roles that you are likely to be applying for. They need to each have a focus on one particular role and the wording needs to reflect what's important for that role. If you have time, the best thing is to do is to tweak or customise your CV for each individual role, taking the lead from the wording used in the job specification.

Please don't lie on your CV – it will catch up with you! You may be able to stretch the truth but a good interviewer will detect this and you may blow your chances. It's best to stick to the truth and then you go in on face value. If you misrepresent yourself and you get found out, it's almost certain you will get kicked out – and severely damage your reputation in the process. In the worst case, if you provide advice which proves not to be the best and further investigation shows your CV is not correct, you could be liable for damages.

Your network

The network of people that you already know is important. Some people think they don't really know many people in the business that they're wanting to get into and this is the same for contracting. However, it is amazing who you DO know.

You can start by looking at your phone. How many people? A hundred, several hundred? So that's a good start – why, because it's not necessarily about those people on your phone, it's about the people that they know and that's the key to your network. It's about letting these people know about the fact that you're looking to go contracting and for them to keep their eyes and ears open. Get them to ask around at work to see if there are any opportunities coming up. Sometimes, it's not necessarily the person on your phone who will have an opportunity, but they sure as hell might know someone who does!

Then, take a look at your email list – different list? They aren't necessarily exactly the same. So there's another source of potential leads. By the time you've looked at Twitter, Facebook, other social networks, your own Social club memberships and acquaintances, you should have quite a healthy list. And remember, it's often about who *they* know.

There is a theory that you are only 6 degrees of separation from being acquainted – by a friend of a friend - to everyone else on the planet –

that is, it's possible to go through a list of 6 people until you find someone who you both know. Which is amazing when you think about it. So, get asking around. You will be truly amazed by what comes back to you. BUT you have to ask in the first place.

I'm not suggesting that your network is the only way you are going to find a job – we will cover that in subsequent chapters – but it is important that you understand who is in your network and that you manage your network going forwards into contracting.

Your day rate

For many, this is a crunch question. How much should I charge myself out at? Typically, people look around the internet, they know a few contractors and what they are earning and they go, "So that's going to be my rate!"

Not quite so fast. True, the best way of working out your rate is to look online and do some searches with some job search engines (such as www.jobsite.com and www.jobserve.com). You enter your criteria, which usually means putting in a role title (which is why working out your branding is so important, see previous section) and some other things like type of role (contracting or permanent), location (to narrow the search down), industry sectors and rate.

Then you get a list of potential contract roles. You should very carefully look at the job descriptions. Some are better than others but if you can genuinely say that you definitely match all the criteria the role is looking for, then you can say that you would have a good shot at somewhere near the rate. But I wouldn't necessarily pitch at that rate. The reason for this is to look at the competition – who are you up against? A potential client is going to look at all the CVs in front of them and work out who they like the look of. Quite often, they will dismiss anyone with little or no contract experience especially when compared with the other CVs that all have plenty of contracting experience. Why? Well, it's down to risk. Are they going to take you on and have you 'cut your teeth' on their project or role? They are potentially taking a risk by employing you.

Unless, that is, you have a reduced rate over the other appplicants. Now, you may place yourself at an advantage. It all depends, of course, quite often on the amount of budget your potential client has at their disposal. If finances are tight, then you might just make the cut as a "well, let's see what sort of person they are".

So, do your research for sure. Work out an average rate for your role and then, my advice would be to pitch your day rate just a little under the average in order to get yourself into your first role. Once you're in contracting, you should quickly set about delivering and getting yourself a reputation. Once you have this in place, then you can look to increase your day rate. To my mind, it's better to get yourself into a role at a lower rate and gain some experience, than sit at home, earning nothing, because you think you're worth more than a client is prepared to pay.

Do the maths. Sticking out for an extra £50/day and taking 4 weeks to get that rate (which is going some!) is going to take you *7 months* to break even against the lower rate job!

Forced transition into contracting from a permanent role

Lots of people (1 in 4 would you believe!) first think about going contracting when they've been made redundant. Quite often, this situation is made a little easier by a pay out, often people are put on 'gardening leave', which means they leave work but are still paid.

I know plenty of people who have been put in this situation and they often react in a similar way. They've got a few thousand pounds in the bank, they're going to take their time making a decision, figure out where they are in their life – an opportunity to really think about what they really, really want to do. Maybe they'll be an artist, retrain to be a builder, get into wine, become a property developer. After all, how hard can it be and this is a great time to take some well earned time out to work it all out.

Hmmm! OK let's get a good dose of reality here. This is a time where it is very easy to wade through a pile of cash. Very easy!

Here's a worked example of a really good friend who was made redundant recently:

October	Finish work
October – January	Taking it easy, no point looking for a job, market flat
January – February	Opportunity to take skiing holiday
February – March	Courses, research and CV writing
March – April	CV honing, Company set up, job hunting, interviews

Mid-April   New job started

End June   1st bill done

End July   1st bill paid

So, 8 months between leaving work and getting paid again.

Makes you think – and look how you start to think in months, not days!! It's like a bit of an early retirement. If you're not careful, it's very easy to take your time over getting back into the market place and by the time you look at your bank balance - WHOAH! Where did all that cash go – PANIC! Quick, make a decision, easy option, go and get a job doing what I did before! And just climb aboard the same hamster wheel in a different place!

So, my advice. Simple. Don't get into this situation if you can help it. If you get the boot from your job, think of any payment as a bonus. Bank it, invest it. You've earned it true enough, but don't blow it. As soon as you're out of the door, and I mean day 1 of your gardening leave if you get it, get your mindset into gear that contracting IS a major option for you and go hell for leather to try this avenue out. DO NOT WAIT until you've ploughed your way through your cash. Get into the mindset of "I am on my own now! It's up to me what I do". Everything that you do from this point on has to be viewed as "Is this going to get me back to a paid job or improve my chances?" If it ain't, don't do it.

Want a holiday? Earn it! Get yourself a contract first, then see if you agree a delayed start date. You've got the contract in the bag – go enjoy that well earned holiday and figure out what you're going to do with all that money you haven't chomped your way through!

Or, if you must navel gaze for a while, plan for 5-6 months worth of money – until you earn again. Your redundancy money can be the opportunity to take time out or it can be a nest egg for the future. Your call.

Outplacement support is often given to outgoing employees these days. They offer services and advice like counselling, CV writing, setting up your own business, interview techniques, and will help you get a new permanent job if you want. I know lots of people who look at these places and poo-poo them. After all, "my CVs brilliant" - isn't it?

Rot. Use them. Take them for all they're worth. Take it all on board. Get the best advice you can on your CV. This is a perfect opportunity to build "Brand You". It's probably the only time in your life you'll get expert advice without paying for it. Do get advice on interview technique and do listen to what they have to say about setting up your own business. One of the best things about these places is that they have office space, internet access, business services. It actually gives you a place to go and get your head together in a place that is full of people who are going through the same experience as yourself. And it's amazing who you meet there. You never know who will be there but take the time to find out. This is the start of building your network. So, is all this moving you towards going contracting? You bet your life. Get in there and suck the advice out of them.

MAKING THE DECISION

So finally, we've got to the point of you making your decision. You've understood in the previous chapters what it takes to become a contractor. You've worked out who you are, your brand, your strengths and weaknesses, you've sorted your CV. So now you are at the point of deciding if contracting is for you.

Making the decision can seem momentous at the time. Only you can know if you have done enough preparation, only you can know if you have the determination to see it through, only you can work out the choices you will have to take to make it work.

However, I always say to people to talk to their business acquaintances, friends and in particular their families. Other people often have experience of this type of working and can advise if you are gong to be the sort of person who is likely to cut it. Your family is a big determining factor in the decision. You and they have to understand how they are going to be impacted and you may not have all the answers when you make the decision. After all, if it was risk-free EVERYONE would be doing it!

Below are my **10 Acid Test Questions** to ask yourself. You really do need to be honest with yourself at this stage. You don't have to answer all questions with a 'Yes' but it will help. Score yourself 1 for a 'Yes', ½ point for a Don't Know and zero for a 'No'.

10 Acid Test Questions you should ask yourself before moving into Contracting
1. Do I think I am going to be able to cope with risk and uncertainty?
2. Is my family behind me and will they be able to cope with me contracting?
3. Am I sufficiently fit to be able to cope with being a contractor?
4. Do I have the right attitude for contracting?
5. Have I really got the skill set that clients are going to buy?
6. Are the rewards for me personally going to be worth the effort?
7. Have I got what it takes to deliver time after time after time?
8. Can I cope with frequent changes in job role, environment and clients?
9. Do I have what it takes to run a company?
10. Do I think I'm going to enjoy being a contractor?

If you're scoring 7/10 or above, I'd say, give it a go. If your score is between 5/10 and 7/10, I would ask yourself seriously if you're cut out for contracting. If you score less than 5/10, or have lots of 'Don't Knows' then put the book down for now, work out what you need to do to get your score up and come back to contracting later – it's not going away!

One thing is for sure, if you don't try, you will NEVER know. What's the worst that can happen? You get into it, it's not for you, you go back to another job, maybe pick up a bit of debt along the way. Big deal? If it is, then maybe you're not cut out for it in the first place.

Making the decision is about giving yourself permission to go to the next steps. You should be in a position where you're saying to yourself "I am prepared to give this a go – now what do I have to do next to get myself a job?"

If this is how you're feeling at this stage in the book, then read on.

The two main things you need to do next are:

1. Put yourself into the market place and
2. decide what kind of trading structure you need to run your business.

These are not necessarily sequential but you do need to do both. In practise, there's only so much running around trying to get a job that you can do. So you will have time and you should spend some time to concentrate on setting up your business.

So, well done you! You've made the decision. That was the hard part really. The rest is relatively straight forward by comparison and I'm going to give you the top tips to get you your first contract and start your new life!

LEAVING YOUR EMPLOYER

I know this section may not apply to all readers. If it doesn't, skip on to the next chapter. If it does, please read this. It's important you manage your exit successfully. For some, it may be the first time you've left an employer, for others, it may have been a while since you last did it.

The way you go about leaving may largely depend on your notice period. Clearly, someone with a week's notice will only have so much they can do compared to someone with a 6 month notice period. Most people have a one month notice period, so I'll assume that and then you can flex the advice according to your circumstances.

I am going to assume that you want to (and you should!) do a professional exit. The reason for this is that "what goes around comes around". If you make a real song and dance as you exit, you never really know who is watching or who you might indirectly impact or who you might come across later in your career. My advice is, even if you hate your job and your employer, take the moral high ground and leave professionally with your head held high.

When should you do it? Should you have a contract in place? Not necessarily. If you have had time to sort your CV, get into the agencies, go to interviews and secure your first role, then great, well done you. But in most cases, you probably won't have this sorted and you need to work out the best timing for you.

There's a section Understanding Seasonality in the Market Place. Read it. There are definitely times not to be trying to find a contract job – like summer and just before and just after Christmas. Only you can determine when the timing is right for your particular circumstance.

Once you've worked the timing out, you should tell your employer as soon as you can. This will give them the best chance of getting someone else in or deciding who will take on your role.

Now you've decided to leave, you should draft your resignation notice. You should keep it simple and to the point and don't be negative. You should book a meeting with your boss and prepare what you are going to say to them ahead of the meeting. You should hand them the letter personally and then have a discussion about why you are going. In this instance, you're looking to be your own boss, earn more, have more flexibility, etc, all the reasons why you've decided contracting is for you. All of these points are positive reasons for moving on. If you can't think of what to say, then try something like this:

"I've been working for you and ABC CO. for the last x years. You've taught me a lot. But now it's time for me to move on to try and learn something new. Thank you for your support. You've been great".

Be prepared for your boss to either try to convince you to stay there and then or ask for time to go away and find out what they might be able to offer you. You then need to know how you are going to respond. If they offer you a promotion or a big rise, it could be tempting to stay – and some people do. But go back to why you got to this point in the first place, examine the reasons why you want to move into contracting and, my advice, stick to your guns! It's a fact that 90% of employees who are "bought" and continue with their employer, leave after a year anyway!

You need to agree a leaving date and the terms of the notice period. You should work during your notice period. If you don't, you are in breach of your contract of employment and your employer can refuse to pay you. Going about leaving professionally may mean that you get offered payment in lieu of notice (PILON), which is brilliant because it allows you to be at home whilst still getting paid – and you can get on with starting up your new business. Gardening leave is another way of achieving this. You get paid and are still legally employed by your employer but you get to be at home and get things going.

You should also ask your employer to provide you with a reference. They don't often provide detailed references but if they refuse to provide a reference, it speaks volumes. In summary, an employer does not have to give a reference unless the employee has a contractual entitlement to one, nor do they have to give a full and comprehensive reference. However, they must provide a true, accurate and fair reference and information should not be provided in malice. They are not allowed to comment on alleged misconduct where there has been no proper investigation and they must not provide sensitive personal information in a reference or provide a reference outside the EU without consent from you.

More often these days, both employer and employee may consider entering into a compromise agreement. In these circumstances, you should always encourage your employer to provide a satisfactory reference as part of the agreement.

Assuming your employer accepts that you are leaving, then let people know you're leaving and when your last day is. Agree a list of things you need to deliver before you go. Work out a handover plan to ensure all your work is managed going forwards and that you've explained to someone the nature of what you've been doing in your role.

This is a handover list that I've used many times. It's a great start to make you think about what you should do to ensure a really great handover to the resource(s) who may be coming in to take on your responsibilities.

10 Key Points for a Great Handover
1.   The responsibilities of the role have been outlined to the incoming resource
2.   The objectives of the role have been agreed for the incoming resource
3.   All key documents have been identified and the incoming resource knows where to find them/has copies of them
4.   All key processes required for the role have been described and the incoming resource has fully understood them
5.   The incoming resource has been trained to use the relevant systems required by the role
6.   All key stakeholders that are involved/interface with the role have been identified and the incoming resource has met with them (where appropriate) and has formed business relationships with them (where appropriate)
7.   All key meetings have been identified and the incoming resource is aware of them and attending them (where appropriate)
8.   All key milestones/timelines have been identified and the incoming resource is aware of them
9.   The incoming resource has been made aware of the broader context in which their role fits
10.   A list of key deliverables, responsibility and delivery date has been agreed

Don't leave before you've left! Be professional to the end. Do not start to talk badly about other people. Don't start taking excessively long lunch breaks. Don't start telling people how much you're going to be earning in your new contract roles. Do work the hours you need to but don't overdo it. Remember, you are about to become self-employed and you need all the time you can get to be getting yourself sorted for that. Work out who you want to stay in touch with and who might be useful to you in the future. Take people to lunch or have a drink with them. Talk to people about what you're going to do – this is the start of you building or expanding your network. Make sure people know how to get in touch with you in the future. If you can, have some business cards made up. You'll be amazed about who knows who and what opportunities might arise as part of these conversations.

Finally, do have some leaving drinks and or a meal. It's always interesting to work out who you're going to invite and even more importantly, who turns up!

GETTING INTO THE MARKET PLACE

Now you've made the decision, you need to get your first contract. There are many ways of doing this. In truth, you will need to pursue ALL potential options, many pathways simultaneously to try to get leads into clients. The most successful way of landing your first contract is to know people who are already contracting and tapping them up to see what opportunities there may be where they are working. But by far the most common route is to use agents who advertise roles. Again, the most common route to find out about contract opportunities is to use the internet to do searches. So this is what we are going to focus on.

Sounds easy eh? You find a few websites, you put in your criteria, you see a contract opportunity you like the look of, you apply and push out your CV and ....guess what, nothing! Yes, this is what happens unless you are very lucky, just happen to have the right skills and the right CV and the guys at the other end just happen to pick up on all this. How many times do you hear of people quoting that they've sent in their CV for hundreds of jobs and heard nothing.

It's because that's not the way it works!

You have to follow up, put the effort in, phone people, talk to people and impress people! This is not going to land in your lap – you have to work for it and I am going to tell you how to maximise your chances.

To get to the top of the pile, it's important you understand the whole process that is happening and where you fit into it.

The overall process is as follows:

1. Client has a contract resource need,
2. Client develops a job specification/description (JD)

3. Client passes JD to their chosen list of recruitment agents

4. Agent posts the role on the internet and other routes

5. People like you apply for the role

6. Agent reviews and selects appropriate CVs

7. Agent sends CVs to client

8. Client reviews CVs and selects people for interview

9. Agent contacts candidates and arranges interview

10. People like you go for interview

11. Client selects the best person to suit their needs and makes offer to you

12. Negotiation takes place

13. Agent gets a contract in place with you

14. You start work with the client

So let's take this one stage at a time and I'm going to tell you what really happens at each level. As part of this, I'm going to tell you how you can maximise the chances of you getting to the top of the pile, to be the person the agents phone first.

1. Client has a contract resource need – this can arise for many reasons –

    *   a change in company strategy or targets means there is a need for a new project, or an expansion in the number of people they need

    *   a change in government regulation means the company has to do something new

    *   a need to develop new products or services

    *   etc – these are just a few examples

    Quite often the client does not have sufficient people in their company to deal with these changes, so they often go down the route of getting temporary or contract resources in. This is great for them because they can hire and fire as required – i.e. they are not taking on additional permanent headcount onto their budget, they don't have to deal with the "red tape" – i.e. no pensions, no need for training or development. Contract resource represents a comparatively easy option for a client. But this assumes that the client is used to dealing with contract staff. Quite a lot of smaller firms don't really do this, so actually, it's the bigger firms where you probably have more chance of landing a contract role. In larger firms, using contract resource is common place. They have so much to deal with, it's just a much easier option. I've worked on big projects for very large clients where 90% of the team have been contractors! Why, because between the contractors, we have the necessary skills to run the project and make it happen on time, we understand the market and quite often, we've done it before. So, we need to make sure the client is engaged but don't need too many permanent staff involved.

Another key requirement for contract staff to be used by a client is that they need to have the money put aside as part of their budget and the budget needs to assume that contract resource will be used.

Despite being a simpler option for a client, contract resource is more expensive than permanent staff in the short term, so there needs to be the budget in place. A key question to ask as you consider the various roles on offer is "does the client have the budget in place and approved?" It doesn't often happen but sometimes, clients can go on a "fishing expedition" to see what resource is out there and to evaluate how much it would be to use contract resource, without having the budget. They then go back to their lords and masters and put a proposition to them to get more money. So, beware.

2. Client develops a role specification/role description

So, you would expect that the client, having got the need for contract resource and a budget in place is going to be really quite explicit about what they want. Truth is, it varies wildly. Some clients are very particular. They take time over the role specification, they consider the skills, experience and attitudes that they need their ideal person to have. They commit this to paper, they get it signed off by the budget owner or executive in charge and then they pass it to their recruitment company.

The other extreme is clients that are under time pressure. They go onto the internet, find a description that will do, or use one they find on their computer, or, worse still, get a contractor to write a job specification (I have done this for clients countless times!) and then they fire it out to an agent with an impossible turn around time and expect quality candidates.

3. Client passes to agent – the client sends the job description (JD) to their agent or agents. Sometimes this is controlled centrally, often by a "Change Management" or "Change Delivery" team or HR. The central team selects the most appropriate agents with whom to lodge the JD. And then they send it out. Client companies often have lists of suppliers that they will deal with who have been selected because they are well known in their business sector and the client has done a deal with them on the amount they are going to charge for their services. This list is most frequently known as the Preferred Supplier List (PSL) and agents who are not on this list should not be representing the client.

The amount a recruitment agent can charge a client varies. For permanent staff, it's usually a percentage of the salary of the recruit. For contract staff, it's almost always a percentage of their daily or hourly rate. This varies between 6% and 20% depending on the type of contractor employed. At the lower end, it tends to be administration staff, secretaries etc. At the other end, it's specialise Programme Directors on big day rates. It's important to understand this because the amount the agent receives can be from £6/day to £200/day. Guess where they are going to put most of their effort? This also helps you to understand why agencies and recruitment companies act the way they do.

4. Agent posts the role on the internet – the agency receives the JD and posts their requirement, usually on the same day. Then, typically, they will look in their database, find some people that they think match the role and, with the person's agreement, they then fire those CVs back to the client, often **within 2 hours**! In the worst cases, they will have CVs back to the client the next day. Again, this is really important that you understand this because when you are looking for a role, and it appears on the internet, you really don't have long to get your CV into the agent. Often, the agent has already put in CVs to the client and this appears to be a brand new requirement to you.

5. People like you apply for the role – so you're looking on the internet, which is the typical place to find roles these days. So where do you look? Well, it depends which industry you're in and what kind of contract market you're in. But there are good generic job search websites out there and in my experience, the best ones are:

Job Site	Website Address	Specialism	Daily email?
Total Jobs	www.totaljobs.com	The UK's largest job site >100,000 vacancies >5,000 companies	Yes
Jobsite	www.jobsite.co.uk	Award winning website 35 industries >50,000 vacancies	Yes
Jobserve	www.jobserve.com	One of the first in the UK Global presence >20,000 vacancies 7m emails sent every week >1m applications processed per month	Yes
Monster	www.monster.co.uk	>5,000 vacancies Part of Monster Global	Yes

Remember that these job boards are exactly that – they are the internet site that the agents use and many agents prefer one particular site. So you shouldn't limit yourself to just looking at one job site.

Check out each site and see which ones fit your situation most. But don't limit yourself to these. There are dozens of specialist online job sites and there may be specific ones for your industry. Ask around. Ask other people in your line of business where they go to look for jobs and add these search engines to your list.

When you go onto these sites, you have the opportunity to register with them. You should do this. It gives you the opportunity to upload your CV and agents can access them directly, which gives you a head start. It also allows you to sign up to a regular (often daily) email list of relevant job opportunities. This is great because it allows you to sift through new jobs and shortlist those where you have a good chance of meeting the requirement.

Typical filters on these websites are:

Industry – Advertising, Media, Engineering etc

Keywords – Project Manager, Communications, Support etc.

Location – input a city around which you want to centre your search (they will usually give you the option to be a certain number of miles from a given place)

Posting date – within the last so many number of days (7 maximum, because it's likely to have gone by then)

Job Type – Contract or Permanent (you wouldn't dare put permie would you!)

Put in your criteria and you're away. You will get a lot of hits that really aren't relevant to you but you have to persevere and examine each potential opportunity in detail. You can add in more specific criteria to reduce the search and make it more focused on your requirements e.g. daily rate.

One of the best is Jobserve, which produces a list of roles matching your search criteria (and way more besides!!) in a ".csv" file, which is a bit like Excel. So when you open it, you can filter out roles you don't want and prioritise it based on location or rate, depending on the completeness of the information in the file.

Also, if you start to look carefully, you can see that there are roles that look quite similar. This happens when the client puts the role with more than one agent. This is important because if you apply for a role via a given agent, you have to stick with them for that role – you have given them permission to act on your behalf for that role. You DON'T and SHOULDN'T change agents as you go through the application process. So look carefully – you will start to build up a list of the agents that are good and those that aren't, and put your applications through the one's you think are good. Another trick that some agencies play is to copy and paste the job role from the appointed agent into their own format and website. They then try to attract attention and if they get people who are interested, they can then forward the details onto the appointed agent at a later stage.

So you select the roles you're interested in, write a brief covering note to the agent, attach your CV, and off you go.

And believe it or not, this is where most people fall down. They expect a torrent of phone calls from agents. You've submitted your CV, you think you're a good match, why wouldn't they call? A good rule of thumb to work with is

"Agencies don't often phone you back!"

If you work with this in mind, you will need to take action to address this and you will not go far wrong. Agents work for clients, not you. Clients pay them, not you. You are an essential part of the overall process but all an agent really wants is your signature on the contract and the agency margin that comes with it.

This is where you need to understand the life of a recruitment agent. They are often paid on a commission-only basis, which means they only get paid if they successfully place someone with a client. The agencies get a 'margin' on the rate at which you get sold into the client. This margin can be as low as 6% of your day rate. On a day rate of £400/day, this equates to £24/day back to the agent or around £2,600 over the life of a 6 month contract, which isn't a great deal of money when you think about it. So, the bigger the role and the higher the rate, the more money they earn. But it is a numbers game too. They will be posting dozens of roles per day. They will be getting tens if not hundreds of applications per day. When they are inundated, they will simply pick out those people that they know, the ones that involve minimum effort and time (and therefore cost), the ones where they know they have the best chance of getting a placement and a signature on the contract.

They may not know a great deal about the role – the good ones do but they are few and far between – but once they are on your side and they have your CV with the client, they do work hard to get to a deal. So treat them carefully – they are your sales-force, selling you in front of the client, so give them every opportunity to do a great job!

Back to the plot, which is you've submitted your CV to the agency. Your job at this stage is to call the agency.

Find a phone number. Sounds easy, but often it isn't straight forward. You need to get to be a bit of a sleuth by scouring the job site emails each day and comparing them – some will have contact details, some don't. Persevere, and get hold of someone to talk to who is dealing with that role. And talk to them about the role, about you and why you are the right person for that role.

Guess what, you're suddenly a sales rep, selling yourself. This is your first interview – with the agency. It's great practise, you get to a point where in 30 seconds, you can recite your pitch and the agent is hopefully going to like what they're hearing.

So a key activity is to prepare your pitch that sells yourself into a particular role.

At this stage, the work you did in the previous sections of the book becomes really useful.

You need to create a pitch which highlights the words and the learning about yourself that came out of your Personal Profile, your SAVE analysis and your SWOT analysis but pitched in relation to the particular role that you're talking to the agent about. So take as much as you can from the role description and in your pitch, say why you are the person that matches the role requirement.

After the pleasantries on the call, the agent at some point is going to give you the chance to answer the question "so tell me a bit about yourself" and this is where your pitch starts.

It's something you can practise up front, you can write it down and you can recite it!

Remember, this is a competitive world – these calls are really important. You should practise your pitch, go in positive but not gushing, sound efficient, alert and bright (which can be difficult early in the morning – but otherwise the role may have gone!), make your pitch and then let the agent sound you out with a few questions.

You should be prepared to answer a whole range of things. Apart from the role content questions (can you do the role, what experience do you have etc) a few are:

10 Key Questions an Agent is going to ask you
1. What's your background?
2. What's your current situation?
3. Why did you move from your last role?
4. What direct, relevant experience do you bring to this role?
5. What kind of role are you looking for and what was your last rate?
6. Why should we put forward your CV to the client?
7. What rate are you looking for?
8. Are you willing to travel/work away from home?
9. Have you applied for this role via another agent?
10. Are you applying for any other roles?

What the agent is trying to work out is if they are going to put you in front of their client and therefore, how much time they invest in you on a call is a useful indicator. They may of course be amassing information about you, knowing that there's no way you match the role they have on offer but that you may be someone they contact in the future about another role. This information should be finding its way onto a central database at the agency, but don't be surprised if it doesn't and don't be surprised if you have to start from scratch with a new agent at the same agency, even when talking about the same role.

It's important that the agent gets a grilling from you too though. You need to know as much about the role as possible and how well the agent is embedded with the client. So, once you've been interrogated, it's time to turn the tables. There are 10 key questions to ask an agent:

10 Key Questions to ask an Agent
1. Have you already submitted CVs?
2. Are you the sole agent for this opportunity?
3. Who is the client? (this is a cheeky one, they often won't tell you)
4. How long is the contract for and are there possibilities for extensions?
5. Where is the contract based and is there the need to travel as part of the role?
6. Will the client pay for expenses?
7. Are there other possibilities with the client for further contract work? (checks how well they know the client and their involvement)
8. What is the client like? (this checks if they really know the client and what their requirement is)
9. What are the more detailed aspects of the role? (again, checking they know the client need)
10. How many other contractors do you have at the client or have you ever placed at the client?

I mentioned previously in this chapter that agents usually get CVs back to their clients within 24 hours of a role coming live. So the question of whether they have already submitted CVs is a key one. If they have, then all is not lost but there's a good chance that the opportunity will not come back to the agent unless all the CVs that the client has received are total rubbish. It does happen but not that frequently.

When the client gives the requirement to more than one agent, you will see the same role appearing more than once. In this case, choose the agency that provides more contact information, like the name of the recruiter. There is nothing more powerful than asking for a specific person when applying for a role.

1. Agent reviews and selects appropriate CVs - After all this effort, you hope that you've impressed the agent sufficiently to get a look in! Hopefully, you can see how you might be able to influence an agent to put your CV to the top of the pile. YOU HAVE TO MAKE SURE ONE OF THEM IS YOURS

2. Agent sends CVs to client - As we mentioned before, it's possible that the agent is only going to put a couple of CVs through to the client. Sometimes the number of CVs submitted is governed by the client especially if they've put the requirement out with a number of agents.

3. Client reviews CVs and selects people for interview – the ideal process at this stage is that the client receives the CV, reviews them, prioritises against a list of requirements, works out which candidates are the most appropriate, makes a decision and gets back to the agent on the same day to arrange interviews. The reality can be somewhat different! A bunch of CVs arrive in the client's inbox. They get printed out and put on their desk....and

there, quite often, they stay for some time. So don't expect that just because the agent has bust a gut to turn round the request that the client is going to act with the same speed! In fact, this can take a very long time. The agent should be all over the client, asking them for an update, cajoling them to interview a specific client. This can and does normally take a few days. So again, don't expect things to happen too quickly. But a top tip is to start a spreadsheet of the roles you're interested in and which one's you've applied for. This allows you to keep track and follow up with the right agencies, which you should do on a daily basis. You can find a format on the website www.breakfreegocontracting.com under the Resources page.

On one occasion, where I had a contract finish on me unexpectedly, and I didn't have a great network in place, and it happened in August (bad time – see Understanding Seasonality in the Market Place), I applied for 90 roles over a two week period. In that kind of situation, you just have to have a spreadsheet to control things, with a copy of the job description, details of the agent, any special notes etc.

4. Agent contacts the candidates and arranges interview – you get a call – yes, it's the ONLY time an agent will definitely call you back! Don't let them go without getting as much from them as possible. Find out more about the client situation, how quickly do they want to hire, has the job spec changed or been refined.

Then, you need to pummel them about the interview itself – here's a checklist:

10 things you need to check about your interview
1. Location of interview
2. Time of interview
3. Who will be in the interview?
4. Contact details for the hiring manager
5. What you are expected to take? (e.g. references, passport/ID, certificates)
6. Dress code – how are you expected to dress?
7. How long will the interview be?
8. What format will the interview take? (review of CV, any tests you will take)
9. Who should you ask for at reception? (could be an assistant for example)
10. Will the client pay for expenses to get you to the interview? (well, you never know! Bit cheeky but if you don't ask, you don't get!)

Prepare as much as you can - Get the job spec and dissect it line by line. Figure out some questions about the role. Work out exactly how you fulfil each part of the job spec and which bits you don't – be honest!

Research the company - Do some research on the company you are going to see. Check out their website and get a copy of their publicly available accounts. Get a sense of their culture, their vision, and ideally as much as you can about the project or the work you will be doing. Seriously, they are going to ask you if you know what they do, so be prepared – it shows you are really interested.

Read and re-read your CV - Go through your CV and work out how you will take the client through it – ask yourself a critical question – what direct, relevant experience am I bringing to this role? Work out against the job spec, which parts of your CV show that you have a great match for what they're looking for.

Mock Interview – if you get nervous in interviews, it can be a good idea to have a mock interview with a friend or business colleague where you can simulate going through what you're going to say about your CV and how you will respond to some made up questions.

10 popular interview questions to be prepared for
1.   Tell me about yourself
2.   What do you think is your predominant style at work?
3.   What are your strengths?
4.   What are your weaknesses?
5.   Why should we hire you?
6.   What are your goals? Or where do you want to be in 3 years time?
7.   Why do you think you want to work here?
8.   Why are you leaving your old job?
9.   How do you work under pressure?
10. Describe a difficult situation that arose at work and how you overcame it

Prepare the things you are going to take - Take a copy of your CV and the job spec with you. Or take a laptop with your CV and the job spec loaded on it or both laptop and hard copies. It just looks professional turning up with something! There is something a little off putting about candidates who wander in to an interview with nothing and sit down and just beam at you. A really good thing to do is take a couple of spare copies of your CV. You just never know when a rushed-off-their-feet client is going to rock up into an interview, without a CV and try to wing it. It does happen. You will instantly be remembered as the person who saved the day and their embarrassment by having a spare copy. If you have been asked to take references or personal ID, then make sure you have these sorted out, printed off where appropriate and in the right suit or bag. Prepare some questions to ask during or at the end of the interview (see below) and write them down, in case your mind goes blank.

Plan your journey, make your own preparations - Work out how long it is going to take to get to the interview and allow some contingency to ensure you get there on or ahead of time. Work out what you're going to wear, the night before, get to bed early, set multiple alarms, ensure you have your eating plans worked out. All this preparation is to make sure that you have as few distractions and dramas on the day of the interview as possible and that you turn up to the interview fresh, alert, nourished and ready for action!!

5. Candidates go for interview – ensure you arrive on time at the right place. Ideally arrive 10-15 mins ahead of the interview to allow you to compose yourself and use the toilet if you have to! Check in with reception and get them to contact the client (on the number you already have with you). If they look at you blankly – don't panic. Phone the number yourself to make sure and see if you can get hold of the client. Be courteous to reception – you never know who they're connected to in the company (especially small companies) and, in general, be well mannered. If you're late, phone ahead and let them know. Sometimes, if you miss your slot, you may have blown it, so find out and don't make a wasted journey.

Once the client picks you up, a firm hand shake is in order – not a bone crusher but not a 'wet fish' either (practise if necessary!), big, confident smile and make good eye contact – as the saying goes, "you only have one opportunity to make a first impression."

So make it a good one. They might ask if you would like a drink – I always accept and see if they make their way to a machine or canteen, then it's a good opportunity to open up a conversation (how your journey down was, how nice the office accommodation is, how easy it is to get there….safe stuff!). Then into the interview. Here's some top tips:

a. Do relax yourself – when you get into the interview room, shake hands with everyone in the room and introduce yourself with confidence. Then settle yourself into your seat – without slouching - and get out your CV, job spec or laptop. Ensure everyone has a copy of your CV and hand out copies as necessary.

b. Smile and look confident – remember they're sometimes as nervous as you might be! They may not be used to conducting interviews or may not have prepared properly. It happens a lot! Don't shuffle about or faff about with your hair, tie, nails or anything else. Don't jiggle your legs up and down during the interview. Keep your arms under control - no 'extravagant' movements! Do keep eye contact but not overly. Don't become distracted by other things either in or outside of the office.

c. Be positive – even if you've had a lousy journey down, put it behind you – you arrived on time and even if the directions they gave you were rubbish, don't get into a negative discussion to kick things off. Showing a positive attitude is the single most valuable thing to demonstrate when you first meet your potential future client.

d. Listen, carefully! – if they start by describing the role in more detail, then LISTEN and listen as hard as you can. Try not to interrupt but do look to comment after they pause. If they ask you if you have any questions, ASK! It shows you have listened and that you are interested.

e. Don't learn a script – try to be yourself, after all, that's what they're buying. Don't deliver answers to questions as if you were reading them. If you have to, then make notes on your CV but it's generally not expected that you will need prompting.

f. Be positive about your previous roles – don't 'diss' your previous roles, focus on the positive and relevant points for the role you're going for.

g. Don't ramble on – be conscious of the time you are talking relative to the amount of time the client is talking. Keep it balanced and be mindful of the time for the interview. You need to use the time effectively to get the points across about your skills, attitudes and experience. Try to speak a little bit more slowly than you would normally and speak clearly.

h. Engage everyone in the room – when answering questions, move your eye contact to others in the room, not just the person who asked you question, but do return your eye contact to the person who opened the question as you finish your response.

i. Dealing with the 'curve ball' – if you get a tough question in the interview that you have difficulty answering, take your time, take a deep breath and show that you're taking time to consider your response. You can sometimes buy more time by asking them to explain the question a little more or repeat it. If you genuinely don't know the answer to a question, say so.

j. Clarify things as you go – remember, the interview is as much about convincing you that the client has a good role for you as it is about impressing the potential client. You should be thinking if this is someone you could see yourself working with. So make sure you are clear about the role, the objectives, the scope and if appropriate, the resources and budget.

k.   End the interview positively – establish when you're likely to hear an outcome and when it is clear that the interview is over, calmly pack everything away and ensure you take everything you brought in with you. Shake hands with everyone as you leave and thank them for their time. Usually the client will escort you back to reception – good time for a little chit chat – and hand your pass back, sign out and with a final big smile and a firm hand shake, stride confidently away. If you phone someone, make sure you're well away from the building – you never know who is around you that might belong to the client, even in a local coffee shop.

The typical structured interview doesn't exist. Every person has their own way. Some organisations can be very process driven in their interview approach in order to ensure consistency of questions and to give everyone an equal chance.

Most of the interviews I have been through, and that I typically use, follow this type of structure:

1.   Introductions to whomever is in the interview room and why they are there
2.   An overview of the company, the current situation and how the project/programme or piece of work fits in
3.   A review of the job description – the role that is to be performed, followed by an opportunity for the candidate to ask any questions

4. The candidate runs through their CV, highlighting key points that are directly relevant to the role, with questioning throughout by the interviewers

5. Final opportunity for all parties to ask any further questions

6. Next steps including expectation on when a decision will be made

Asking questions is key. In your preparation, just make sure you have a few questions to ask during the interview and leave some to ask at the end. It leads to all sorts of good conversations and shows you're interested.

10 great questions to ask during or at the end of an interview	
a.	As a contractor, how would I meet/exceed your expectations?
b.	What excites you about coming into work on this project/for this company?
c.	What are the most enjoyable and least enjoyable parts of the role?
d.	Is there likely to be more contracting work available in the future?
e.	Are there opportunities for more senior roles in the future?
f.	How would you describe the work culture here?
g.	What do you think will be the most important issues that we will face?
h.	How will this project/role contribute to the overall goals of the business?
i.	Do you have any doubts about whether I am suited to this role?
j.	When will I hear if I've been successful and when will the role start?

If the agent has indicated that the client will pay expenses, it is a good move to get clarification on what is covered and not covered. You do need to judge this though. If the interview has gone well, it's worth pursuing. If you think you are borderline, you can always pursue via the agent at a later date, when you've been offered the role. Expenses are a great negotiating point and can help you achieved an enhanced daily rate. See Section 12 below.

While the individual face-to-face interview is by far the most common place type of interview for contractor positions, there are other ways of carrying out interviews and it is equally important that you prepare for these too.

Telephone interview – when faced with a large response to a given role, some clients use telephone interviews to narrow down the field of applicants rather that just relying on gut instinct when sifting through a pile of CVs. It's cost effective and quick. Interviews last about 15 minutes but you can be faced with the same questions as you would expect at a normal interview. The focus is typically on the job spec and why it appeals to you. The classic "why should we choose you to come to interview over the other candidates?" question is bound to come up, so be prepared for that one.

Some tips are:

- Don't talk too quickly even though time is limited
- Prepare some bullet points about the things you want to get across
- Prepare some questions and write these down so you can reference them easily
- Choose a quiet location where you are not going to be disturbed
- Compose yourself before the call
- Concentrate and listen to what is being said - if you're not sure, ask them to repeat what they said

Group interview – this is very rarely used for contractor roles in my experience but it's worth touching on it just in case. There are the same messages as above about being prepared, arriving early but in these situations, you have to be ready to deal with anything!

Clients using this method of interview are primarily looking to see how you interact with others, so it's important to be courteous and polite but clear and firm. You need to turn up your listening skills to 10.

In this type of interview, it is commonplace for the client to set a task that must be performed by the group or the client can split the interviewees into groups to compete against each other. If the client sets you a task, be absolutely clear about what the task is and ask questions to seek clarification – but not too many and make sure you don't come over as a smart alec. Often, clients are looking for leadership skills in this setting, so be assertive but not aggressive, look for consensus among the group, split the task up between people, challenge constructively and make sure everyone is included in the discussions. Sometimes, you can be asked to prepare a short presentation about a given topic to feedback to the group. In this situation, use your judgement, but it can be useful to be seen to be taking the pen – the person with the pen is definitely in charge - and summarising as you go. You can then choose to either present the findings yourself, as you wrote them, or be seen to delegate this to someone else.

Be positive and try to enjoy the experience – quite often, you learn a lot about yourself in these exercises and often, the client will provide feedback there and then or will have someone who acts as an observer and is trained to advise on performance during group tasks.

This is a quick skim through what can be quite a complex situation. If you are faced with this type of interview, try to glean as much as you can from the agent and the client about the way in which they are going to conduct the interview.

Competency based interview – these can also be called structured or behavioural interviews. They are the most complex form of interview and demand a different level of preparedness. It is extremely unusual to see this approach used for selecting contractors but I've included it here to ensure you understand what is likely to happen if the client does adopt this approach. Clients usually have a pre-agreed list of questions that serve to check your behaviour in given circumstances. You are often expected to back up your behaviour with examples from your work or personal experience. Clients often dig down into the detail of your response. A typical list of competencies that can be checked is as follows:

- Adaptability
- Compliance
- Communication
- Conflict Management
- Creativity and Innovation
- Decisiveness

- Delegation
- External awareness
- Flexibility
- Independence
- Influencing
- Integrity

- Leadership
- Organisational awareness
- Resilience and tenacity
- Risk taking ability
- Sensitivity to others
- Team work

There are a whole range of questions that can be asked, depending on the way in which the client decides to structure the interview. Some questions may not be specifically related to a specific skill. The client may start off with some generic questions like "How do you manage upwards?"

Within the framework of competency-based interviews, there are specific questions that are worked out beforehand and these are used across all candidates, so that there is a fair scoring system. Some example questions are:

"Tell us about the biggest change you had to deal with."

"Tell us about a time when you went against company policy."

"What is the worst communication situation that you have had to deal with?"

"Give us an example where you were unable to deal with a difficult member of your team.

"What big decision did you make recently? How did you go about it?"

"Give us an example of where you did not delegate when you could have done."

"If we gave you a new project to manage, how would you go about it?"

"Describe a time when you failed to sell an idea you knew was the right one."

"What would you do if your boss asked you to do something illegal?"

"Tell us about a situation where you had to get a team to improve its performance."

In answering each question, you need to demonstrate that you have the right skills by using examples based on your prior experience.

Before the interview, clients will have worked out a scoring plan depending on how you answer each question. They will be looking for positive and negative indicators so you will often see clients ticking or scoring you as you go through the interview. You score higher depending on how well the client thinks you have demonstrated your skill in each specific area.

You can see that these are tough questions to answer and there are so many possible questions for each competency that it is impossible to know what you're going to be asked.

So I hope you can see that this is the most complex type of interview. From the client side, it demands a competency framework, structure, organisation, up front planning and a good deal of time – which is ultimately why you're unlikely to see this style of interview used to select contractors.

However, if you have to go through one of these, the messages are very similar to the other types of interview in terms of ensuring you have the best chance of success.

You must prepare – find out which competencies they are likely to test you on, if you can. If the client or the agent won't tell you, then dissect the role description and work it out yourself. Work out some questions that might be asked, then go through your CV, go through your experiences and identify some good examples that would be relevant for each competence area.

Develop each of these scenarios and remember to describe the situation you found yourself in, describe and focus on what YOU did, how you did it and why you did it. Finally, focus on the result or the outcome, describe how it was successful and importantly, write down what you learned form the whole experience.

This takes time, but you will go into this type of interview well prepared. Trying to think all this through off the top of your head, would be incredibly difficult and not deliver the focused response that the interviewers are looking for.

In all situations, do try to get some feedback from the client as to how you got on and how you came over to them. This is incredibly useful information. Often we don't like hearing that we didn't quite have the right skills or experience but if you get feedback that says you weren't enthusiastic enough, then that's something you can put right next time.

Often, the agent will phone you (yes, they're interested in you now because you've got potential pound signs above your head!) to ask how it all went and may have already received some feedback for you. In any case, it's a good thing to be prepared for. Try not to be negative about your interview experience but do be honest about how you think you did. If you think it went well, ask the agent to find out when the client is going to make a decision and if they haven't yet got feedback about you, ask them to get some from the client. Even if you didn't think the interview went too well, the agent is potentially someone who would look to put you in another role, and if you've been selected for interview by one client, it can mean that your CV goes to the top of the pile next time.

Finally, remember that the interview is a key part of the selection process but not necessarily the only means of selection. The client will be taking your day rate, your experience, your location, and many other factors into consideration before finally making their decision.

6. Client selects the best person to suit their needs and makes the offer – we are going to assume you got the role – well done you!!

This is how it works. The client will contact the agent directly after the interview. They have made their mind up and they want you to start as soon as possible – generally. The agent will confirm the details of the offer and effectively make a contract between the agent and the client. In some instances, the client will be willing to contract with an individual, although this is getting more and more rare these days. Clients want to distance themselves from any liabilities and problems that could be caused by a contractor, so they use agents in the vast majority of instances.

7. Negotiation takes place – or not as the case may be! You've been offered the role and now it is up to you to work out if the offer you've been made is adequate for you or not. If they are offering you the rate they advertised, it can be tricky trying to get more. And you should have managed expectations with your agent at the outset. If they've put you forward at a rate higher than the advertised rate, then you have an opportunity to negotiate.

But if you feel like you had a strong empathy with the client and you might be able to push for more, then go ahead and ask your agent to go back to the client and make the request. Often agents are reluctant to do this because they took on the role at the advertised rate. Most clients going through an agent expect the cost of a contractor to be fixed. It's easier for them to budget, being just a simple multiple of the number of days worked. So this is entirely your call.

However, a way of getting your rate up is to negotiate expenses. The client can keep your rate the same but offer you expenses and effectively 'hide' the increased cost, while you effectively receive an increased day rate. They can hide this because expenses are usually dealt with differently in a business, and are at the discretion of the hiring manager to sign off. Expenses can be put through other budgets, sometimes they are managed centrally.

The question is, how far can you stretch this? The answer is not too much. You can try to negotiate a fixed rate per day for expenses, a capped rate per month or go forward on a cost incurred basis, in which case, you will charge based on invoiced amounts that you can submit. The key to how much is to work out what's fair. You cannot be seen to be treated in a preferred way compared to employees. Also, this is where contractors are treated differently to consultants! Consultant expenses are usually part of the overall contract agreed with big firms, so they expense everything at cost. Hence you will see them inhabiting the Marriott and Hilton hotels without batting an eyelid and having restaurant meals out, with plenty of drinks and charging the lot through. A top tip is when you make friends of these guys, and you go out with them in an evening, they will often pick up the tab!!

So what is fair? Your expenses are usually travelling (from your registered office to your place of work), accommodation and subsistence (daily allowance). Take me as an example. I do a return rail trip into London each week, use the tube mainly, rarely taxis, live in an inexpensive hotel for 4 nights a week and eat moderate meals during the week, maybe take the client out once a fortnight. For that, my costs are £400/week - £500/week. To cover these costs, I could agree a daily expense allowance of £100/day, I could agree a fixed or capped expense arrangement of say £500/week (£2,000/month) or I could agree that I would charge expenses at cost.

In my experience, clients seldom like to cover contractor expenses at more than £50/day. But I have had a client that paid for a rental apartment and my travel costs but not my subsistence (unless I was taking them out for a meal!!), which regularly amounted to £1,800/month – no not just the meals!!

For travel, if you go by train or plane, it's easy. You charge for your rail/air fare and keep copies of the receipts. If travelling by car, you would charge the client at the same rate as a permanent employee. This is often different from what you claim back from the tax man. A lot of clients allow their staff to claim at between 20p/mile and 25p/mile. The taxman allows you to claim travel back at 45p/mile for the first 10,000 miles and then 25p/mile over this mileage. So you would invoice the client at 20-25p/mile but charge the expense back through your company at 45p/mile. This has the effect of reducing your profit and means you end up paying less tax – which is good!

For accommodation, if you stay in a hotel or B&B then this is pretty straightforward to charge as an expense. You get a receipt each week and charge through. Again, check with the client on allowable expense limits that a permanent employee would receive. They are sometimes capped at a daily limit. Also, check with your client if they receive discounts at any hotels. You should be able to benefit from better rates if you mention you're working for the client. A further top tip is if you think you are going to spend a long time in a hotel – like 6 months or more – pick a hotel that has a good reward scheme. It may sound ridiculous but I know someone who stayed in a Marriott for 9 months, picked up the points, had the choice of any bedroom they wanted, including suites, for the basic price, had free wine on arrival, fruit, newspapers and in the end had so many points, they went to the Cayman Islands for a week FREE!

For subsistence, you can legitimately include breakfast and evening meals but do check with the client that they are happy to cover this expense and again check the limits that apply to permanent staff and ensure you don't go over this limit. I personally don't charge for lunches either to the client or to my company, given that I have to eat to live. But you can legitimately charge many expenses into your company – see Company Expenses section later.

Clients will need the original receipts to process an expense claim. It is important that you keep a copy for your own records so that you can show actual expense incurred in running your business to the taxman.

So the moral of the expenses story is, when you eventually land the contract with the client, always, always, always check with the client what you can charge for and what the limits are. Don't assume anything and don't ever try and fiddle your expenses. Remember, you will be doing well if you can claim expenses so don't push it.

Agent gets a contract in place with you – the agent then phones you with the good news. So you feel pretty good – you've been offered a role. Time to celebrate? Not quite yet. In this industry, 'It ain't over till the fat lady sings'. Anything can change – the client can change their mind, the job can disappear, someone can have an accident that completely changes the whole situation. No, the fat lady sings when you get ink (or click send) on your final, agreed contract. There's still a way to go yet. The agent will put their standard contract in front of you for the kind of role you have secured. It is up to you to work out if this has all the necessary parts to it and for you to work out if you are happy to sign it. This is one time where you do have to read the small print. There are some key things to watch out for:

10 things to check on your Contract
1.   Start and end date are defined
2.   The rate is defined and is correct
3.   Payment frequency is defined and how you go about recording your time/getting your time approved
4.   Invoicing process is defined (a booking code or contract reference number needs to be clearly defined)*
5.   The description of services provided by you is accurate and you believe you can deliver them
6.   A standard working day is defined – the number of hours you are expected to work
7.   Holidays and how many you can take, any restrictions that you need to be aware of and the procedure for agreeing them is defined
8.   Overtime is defined as well as if you get paid for this or not
9.   Location and place of work are clearly defined
10. Expenses and what you're covered for and how you claim them is defined (see separate section on this)

* See advice on invoicing under Running your Business Month to Month

It can be very useful to have someone else have a look over the contract. They can often see things that you can't or don't see – as, by this stage, you're just keen to get started and will sign almost anything!! Once you're happy with the contract, then you can sign/click send. The agent should gain a signature internally from their own agency (usually a Director) and then finally send you a hard copy of the signed contract.

It's over right? I can celebrate? Maybe not quite yet. It depends on your circumstances and the client/contract. In some cases, you will need to be checked out. This can involve getting CRB (Criminal Records Bureau) checked.

The CRB check has now been replaced by the DBS – the Disclosure and Barring Service, but people still call it the CRB check. The service basically helps employers make safer recruitment decisions by carrying out background checks on individuals who are applying for jobs. The service allows employers to access the criminal record history of potential employees. It is done with your full co-operation and involvement. Employers can ask you to undergo a standard/enhanced/enhanced with a barred list check, depending on what kind of job you are applying for. In most situations the standard check is used. This checks out your convictions, cautions, reprimands or warnings and includes both 'spent' and 'unspent' convictions. You receive a form to fill in, which basically asks a few personal questions. You sign the form and send it off to the DBS. They then search the Police National Computer and check any records held by the Police. The outcome is then sent to both you and the prospective employer. The DBS promise to get 95% of standard checks completed within 2 weeks of receiving a completed application form. So just be aware that this can hold up proceedings when you apply for a role and the client insists on putting you through this process.

Another complication can be caused if you are not a UK citizen. In this instance, there may be additional checks that the agent will need to take – more to prove your identity. The DBS cannot access criminal records held overseas and may need to contact the relevant Embassy or High Commission. It is also up to the potential employer to check if you have permission to work in the UK.

A final word of caution, watch out for Procurement getting involved. It happens more and more these days. They check the contract over and the deliverables and make sure the business is hiring contractors for all the right reasons. Naturally, ask someone to check a contract and they will want to find something to comment about. It's their job, right? Even the most innocuous comments can take days to resolve, so keep on it. Check Procurement have added their signature, otherwise, the contract isn't going anywhere.

I would recommend giving the client a call to keep them up to speed with how the contract signature is going. Sometimes you might need the client to give their agent a kicking to keep things on track – especially if you know that the client is really keen to get you on board and has some tight deadlines to meet.

But assuming this is all in place and you've signed your contract, then you're pretty much home and dry and it's now time to uncork the champagne!

8. You start work with the client – so you have two approaches here – get prepared or don't! I would advise the former as you might expect. I think it's important to keep the client in the loop as to what's happening to their star recruit.

    You should always call prior to arriving on site. This is to ensure everything is still on track from the client perspective. They can usually do useful things like get you a desk, laptop/PC, access to shared drives, access to the site, security passes, to name but a few. It's also a chance to find out a few details about where you should be and when you should arrive on Day 1 and who you should ask for etc. You should absolutely confirm the most appropriate dress code. I said it before but, you only have one chance to make a first impression – there's nothing worse for a bloke than turning up on Day 1 without a tie, when everyone else is wearing one! For ladies, nothing too showy, hem line is critical! You should have picked this up as you walked in to your interview and checked out the people walking around the office but it is always worth checking.

Finally, do take along a note book, pen, phone, and ideally a laptop. If the client hasn't quite got you sorted from an IT perspective, it shows great initiative to have brought your own means of doing work. Do be careful about what you store on your personal computer. Ensure you have virus protection and encryption software if you are going to store client information on your own laptop.

As you walk in, big smiles all round, big confidence, shoulders back, walk tall – you're the new team member and people are generally going to want to like you. You're there because they were short of resource, or didn't have the right kind of resource or they have someone move on. In any case, you're needed! Clients don't hire external resources for the hell of it!

Be careful not to come across as the big "I am" – unless you genuinely are! Do not flaunt your rate and be careful about discussing your personal circumstances – jealousy is a terrible thing and can do strange things to people.

Check the team dynamics around you. You need to pick up on how busy everyone is and match this with your own way of working – no point clearing off for an hour's lunch if everyone looks under pressure. However, I am a fan of setting standards in the first week. So if you can leave on time, then do. Find out what the typical time of departure is on Friday's. Some clients are ok with contractors leaving a bit early to get home, if they live a couple of hours away. Some most definitely are NOT! So suss this out quickly and get it right!

So there you have it, you're in! The rest is up to you. Be attentive, put the effort in and enjoy pulling in your day rate in what is hopefully a rewarding environment. There's more later on starting out and managing your first contract but first, we need to look at which business structure is best for you.

SETTING YOURSELF UP IN SELF-EMPLOYMENT

As I mentioned at the end of the previous chapter, while ever you're having 'fun' talking to agents and getting yourself a job, you do need to think about what kind of business structure you need going forward. Oh dear, I can almost feel that 'ostrich moment' as a whole load of you bury your heads in the sand. This is the bit you don't want to know about, right? Or the bit that seems just that little bit too hard.

That's exactly what I thought when setting up and actually, it's really not that bad at all. In fact it can be really quite easy. The simple way to work this out is get a good accountant and let them sort it all out. They will ask you some questions about what you expect to earn, then they'll work out the best structure for you, set up your accounts, your books and tell you what forms you have to fill in and when. Easy. It will cost you but you can delegate the whole process to them.

Yes, but I think it's worth understanding a little about the decision making process about what kind of company to set up so you know you're getting the right advice. This is part of you taking some control over your future, about you understanding about company structures and business in general. So it will not do you any harm to know this stuff! In my experience, I have sometimes not had what I consider to be the best advice and relying on your accountant too much is not necessarily the right thing to do.

Choosing the Best Company Structure

So let's start with the basics. There are four choices facing a new contractor. You can be a Sole Trader, Director of a Limited Company, in Partnership, a Partner in a Limited Liability Partnership or you can delegate a lot of responsibility for running your business affairs to what is called an Umbrella Company. Ultimately, the decision depends on a number of factors that will be personal to you and your situation but it does impact how much effort you need to put in to running your company and the amount of tax you will pay.

As a simple rule, to maximise your income (i.e. pay least tax), then forming a limited liability company is the most attractive, where you typically take home over 80% of what you earn. For a sole trader, in similar circumstances, your take home earnings would be 73% and for an umbrella company the equivalent take home would be 65% of your earnings.

For some of you, I know this will be the clinching argument, but stay with me and look at the options. Let's do a quick overview and then dive into more detail on each.

Sole Trader	
Definition	A company started and run by one individual, where there is no legal distinction between the owner and the business (which means you are personally liable for all the company's debts) but you can take all the profits of the business, once you've paid tax on them.

Pros	Cons
- Easy to start up	- You are personally liable for all the debts of the business (so you could lose your house)
- Subject to fewer regulations	- You are taxed on the whole of the profit
- You have full control over all business decisions and accounts	- You will pay normal Tax and National Insurance contributions
- You can easily stop the business (just stop trading)	- You have to registered as self-employed
- You take all profits in the business	- You send in your own self-assessment tax form
- You can register for Flat Rate VAT scheme that allows you to keep some of the VAT you charge to clients (see later)	-

Limited Company	
Definition	A limited company is a business that has been registered and ensures that its owners have limited liability (i.e. you are NOT personally responsible for all the debts of the company). The business is owned by shareholders and operated by directors, so it's likely you will be a Director and a shareholder.

Pros	Cons
- You pay less tax	- You have to complete an annual tax return and file company accounts
- You have no personal liability for the company's debt (so they can't come and take your house off you)	- You have to pay Corporation Tax (currently 20% for companies with a taxable profit of less than £300,000)
- You can claim a wider range of expenses	- You are likely to need an accountant (costs between £750 - £1000 per year)
- You can register for the Flat Rate VAT scheme that allows you to keep some of the VAT you charge to clients (see later)	

Pros	Cons
- You choose how much you pay yourself, which can significantly reduce the amount of tax you pay	
- You control the amount of National Insurance payments (currently 12% of salary) you make above £7,676	
- Companies prefer to deal with Limited Companies (it reduces their liability if things go wrong)	

Limited Liability Partnership (LLP)

Definition	A relatively new structure (first set up in 2000), it is a legal entity (like a limited company) where the LLP is responsible for the debts of the business and not the partners – i.e. there is limited liability (so if it all goes wrong, your personal assets, like your house, are protected).

Pros	Cons
- There is no Corporation Tax or Capital Gains Tax to pay	- LLPs must file accounts at Companies House
- Profits are distributed gross to the Partners according to any agreement written down and tax is paid as required by you as an individual	- If profits exceed £200,000, the remuneration of the highest paid partner must be disclosed
- No employers National Insurance is payable (but you yourself will have to pay it!)	- Compared to a Limited Company, you pay more tax in an LLP (at up to 40%/50% on the whole of the profits compared to 20% corporation tax on net profits i.e. post allowable expenses)*
- You are not responsible for the actions of other partners	- You have to be registered as self-employed

Pros	Cons
- No restriction on the number of partners	- You send in your own self-assessment tax form
- LLPs can own assets, which partnerships cannot	- The LLP is still liable for VAT over the minimum VAT threshold (currently £79,000 turnover – at May 2013)

* *if you take the overall tax position, to pay the same overall amount to a Limited Liability Partner compared to a Limited Company Director, you would have to make more profit in the Limited Company, if the Director takes the equivalent salary to a LLP Partner. Bottom line is, it all depends on how you take the money out and how much profit you are likely to make, so my advice is seek advice if you think an LLP might work for you.*

Umbrella Company	
Definition	A company that provides payroll services and acts as an employer to professional contractors who work under a fixed term service contract, often via an Intermediary (e.g. an agency) to a Client. It manages all invoicing, taxes are collected via PAYE and expenses are allowable (for things like travel, meals and accommodation)

Pros	Cons
- You don't have to do much paperwork	- You have to pay a fee for this service (can be up to 9% of the contract value)
- You often get covered for Liability Insurance as part of the fee	- You can't claim the same level of expenses as you can in a limited company
- You can get paid weekly	- You will pay more tax
	- Umbrella companies sometimes have a minimum contract length

The main two options that contractors typically consider are the Limited Company or Umbrella Company routes, so we will consider these in more detail next. If you want more information on sole trader businesses, visit

https://www.gov.uk/business-legal-structures/sole-trader

and for Partnerships go to

https://www.gov.uk/business-legal-structures/limited-partnership-and-limited-liability-partnership or talk to an accountant.

Setting up a Limited Company

This is genuinely not difficult to do. There are over 400,000 Limited Companies set up every year. There are over 3 million Limited Companies in the UK. Over 90% of all incorporations, as they are called, are set up via 'formation agents' because it is really easy and quick you can access a list of formation agents via the Companies House website at:

www.companieshouse.gov.uk/toolsToHelp/formationAgents.shtml

but it is very easy and quick and cheaper to do it yourself.

There are two main types of limited company – one limited by shares, the other limited by guarantee. The limited company limited by shares is generally the best option for contractors.

The main steps you need to take to set up a limited company are listed below (there follows a more detailed explanation of each step but what I'm trying to show you here is that there really isn't that much to it).

You have to do these things:

1. Decide on a Company Name, decide who the Directors are (including share allocation) and register (or incorporate it) with Companies House
2. Set up a Business Bank Account
3. Within 3 months, let HMRC know that you've set up a Company and register for Corporation Tax

You might have to do these things:

4. Register for VAT if you think your annual turnover (sales or revenue) is going to exceed £79,000 (limit at May 2013).
5. Register for PAYE if you are going to be an employer

Ongoing, you will have to do these things (but I'll cover this later under Managing your Limited Company)

6. Manage ongoing activities of running a Limited Company
    a. Manage quarterly VAT returns
    b. Submit annual self-assessment tax return
    c. Submit annual Company Accounts and Corporation Tax Returns
    d. Manage payment of Corporation Tax within 9 months of year end
    e. File an annual return to Companies House within 9 months of year end
    f. Manage monthly payroll
    g. Manage invoicing
    h. Manage insurances

Incorporating a Limited Company with Companies House

Companies House is the UK registry of all Companies and their corporate information, including details about shareholders, company address and turnover and is part of the UK Government. It ensures that Companies submit the relevant company information required by law under the Companies Act 1985 to 2006. The main functions of Companies House are to:

- incorporate and dissolve limited companies;
- examine and store company information delivered under the Companies Act and related legislation; and
- make this information available to the public.

Anyone can access information held in Companies House, with a charge being made for access to more detailed information. All Companies have to file an Annual Return and submit Annual Company Accounts to Companies House.

To register with Companies House, you need to have the following information

- Company Name and Address
- Officer Details (Director and Secretary)
- Share Capital and Shareholder Details
- Payment

and that's it! So let's look at these steps in more detail.

Deciding on a name for your Business

This really doesn't take long to sort out but it is incredibly important that you do think through a good name for your company. The safest thing to do is to call your company after your own name. So you can use your initials or your name, then again, the simplest thing to do is call yourself ABC Associates. This implies to a client that you are the main driver behind the company but you also have a network of people that you leverage on. You can choose ABC Consulting or ABC Consultants but be sure that you have the necessary experience and qualifications behind you before doing this. I would avoid going for 'zingy' or 'racy' titles such as 'White Lightning Associates' or 'Hassle Free Consulting'. You are just opening yourself up to abuse and potential ridicule. You also need to think about how you will look representing your company in the future. So if a white haired, experienced, demure, businessman turns up with a card that says 'Go Get 'Em Associates', it might not fair too well with a client.

Your company name does depend on what you are trying to achieve though. It depends if you're going to be happy pursuing a 'one-man band' approach or trying to build a company and a brand. So you need to consider this at the outset.

Other things to consider are the place you live, the name of your house, your favourite composer/band/author but choose something that you can feel empathy with. Remember, this name could be with you for a long time – so put the effort in and get it right.

Once you have chosen your ideal name, you need to do a couple of checks. First is log on to www.companieshouse.gov.uk and check that the name you have chosen is not already registered. Go to their WebCHeck listings of companies – it's free to check. If it is, you cannot use that name but you can go for something very close to it. One of my companies is called Rapid Effects Ltd, but there are many other companies with similar names to mine – Rapid Effect Signs Ltd, Rapid Effort Ltd, Rapide Consulting Ltd. So you could set up a company called Rapide Associates Limited and you'd probably be ok. The only thing that Companies House stipulate is that you should be careful when using any words in the name of your company that are 'sensitive' and what they mean by this is that the name should not convey any elevated status or imply a link to the Government or cause offence. In some of these cases, you have to get further permission to be able to use certain words. Some relevant examples are the words Agency,

Association, Group (unless you can name at least two other companies that are part of the Group), Holdings (unless the company satisfies the criteria for being a Holdings company), Institute or Institution (unless you are conducting research at the highest level), International (unless you can prove that the business will do a significant part of its business overseas) and National. There is a complete list of sensitive words on the Companies House website. It's worth having a quick flick through:

http://www.companieshouse.gov.uk/about/gbhtml/gp1.shtml#appA#

The second and arguably just as important check is to type in the name of your company into Google and into a web address. The Google check will be of interest to see what comes back especially if a client was to type in your company name. Check to see that there isn't already another company elsewhere (e.g. the US) where your company name is already being used. If it is, look at their web address and see if you are likely to have internet traffic diverted to them rather than to you e.g. if they are trading as ABC Associates and using the website www.abcassociates.com then it may not be a great idea to set up and register ABC Associates using the website www.abcassociates.co.uk.

It is getting more and more difficult to find available website names to go with good company names. There are plenty of companies out there that have registered thousands of good names and web site addresses and are more than willing to sell you these.

Once you've done these checks and everything looks ok, you can go ahead and register with Companies House (or have your accountant do it) and then register and buy your company web address. If you can, then it's best to reserve the .co.uk and .com versions of your address. This potentially stops people buying the site that you didn't buy and then trying to sell it to you or, worse, snaffling a load of traffic/visitors that erroneously typed in the wrong web address.

A top tip at this stage is to think carefully about which sector you are going to register your business in. Companies House classify companies into a number of generic business types according to their principal business activity. They call this the SIC code (Standard Industrial Classification). At the end of each year, every limited company has to submit an Annual Return form (AR01) to Companies House. It doesn't take long but when you first fill it in (at the end of your first year), you have the chance to determine your principal activity. Typically, a generalist contractor might fit under Management Consultancy (SIC Code 70229) or IT Consulting Services (SIC code 62020). It can be a shrewd move to register under these for one reason. When you get your company running and earning some income, you may get to a point where you will charge VAT (current threshold is £79,000). There is a good scheme that the HMRC offer called the Flat Rate VAT scheme or FRS. We cover this later in the VAT chapter and it depends on which sector you're registered in as to how much you can benefit by using this scheme. Skip ahead to the chapter and work out how you're best registering your business.

Deciding on your Company Address

Most people use their residential address as their Company address. This is generally fine but you might need to check out the following. Ensure you don't have any restrictive covenants on your house deeds. This can stop you trading from home but generally only if someone else knows about the covenant. You may need to check with your mortgage provider. Sometimes there are restrictions but as long as you write to them and let them know, you should be fine – if they even acknowledge the letter in the first place! There are no council tax implications but you may be able to offset some office costs against your tax bill (but beware, the tax man can claim back a proportion of your house capital gain in the future if you do this). Finally, if you're expecting many visits from clients, you need to consider the impact of any additional traffic on your neighbours.

The alternatives are to use your accountants address or use a PO Box number, to maintain anonymity of your home address if you wish to remain private. Companies House won't let you use a PO Box without it being attached to a physical location though. The registered office address must be in the UK in order to register the company with Companies House.

Deciding on Officer Details

This isn't as scary as it sounds. You have to decide who is going to run the Company. You must have at least one Director. A Director is legally responsible for running the company properly and must be at least 16 years of age (and you can't be a disqualified Director!). The only other choice you need to make is whether you are going to have a Company Secretary. Company Secretaries are required to ensure all the legal obligations required by the company are carried out. For a contractor, this includes ensuring there are regular meetings and an annual meeting, taking minutes and actions at these meetings, making sure dividend payments are made and filing the annual return to Companies House. You don't need a Company Secretary because, as a Director, you can do all these things yourself or have an accountant do them but some contractors do have one to share the load of invoicing and administration. You can also make the Company Secretary a shareholder too, which means they are entitled to dividend payments.

Quite often, the Company Secretary can be your wife or husband or partner. As long as they are carrying out their duties, you can share some of your tax burden – do be careful on this though. See the chapter on S660, which tells you about the rules and regulations on sharing dividends in husband and wife teams.

Share Capital and Shareholder Details

When you register a company, you need to make what's called a 'statement of capital'. This is the number of shares the company has and their total value and the names and addresses of the shareholders. The full meaning of 'Ltd' or 'Limited' after a company name is a private company limited by shares.

Not as hard as you might first think – why? Because you make it up, that's why. It's entirely up to you how many shares you have in the company and who owns them. A new company must have at least one share. Typically, a new company will start with Ordinary £1 shares and have 100 or 1,000 shares. I'm not going to go into detail on other types of shares as this is unlikely to be needed for a simple contractor company. If you think you need something more complex (such as Preference Shares, Cumulative Preference or Redeemable shares), then talk to an accountant.

Who gets these shares is entirely up to you. Often, it is the Directors only, sometimes, you might have investors, in which case they might have some shares allocated to them as a result of the money they are putting into the company up front. But you do not have to issue all the shares and you can keep some back in case you want or think that you might want to bring other Directors in as share holders at a later date.

This makes it relatively simple and relatively cheap – yes, you do have to pay the company for the shares that it has issued to you.

The shareholders are the owners of the company. The shareholders appoint Directors to run the company on their behalf but in the case of most new contractor businesses, the owners and Directors are one and the same.

The primary benefit of being a shareholder is that you can be paid dividends from the company's profits, which is a more tax efficient way of getting money out of the company than being paid a salary and paying tax through PAYE. More on dividend payments later.

Payment to Set Up a Private Limited Company

You can do all the above and set up your company online via the Companies House website, which will cost you £15, you can fill in a form (IN01) and post it to them, which costs £40 for 8-10 day service or £100 for same day service, you can use a formation agent (there's a list of them on the Companies House website) and they can charge anywhere between £4.99 and £100 in addition to the incorporation fee – but look closely at the service you are getting for the money you are spending, or you can use an accountant and they will often go via a formation agent.

And it really is as easy as that. There are some scary terms used in the setting up of a company but actually, it's very easy. This is also the very exciting point at which you decide what to call yourself in your new position. You can be a Director, a Managing Director, a Chief Executive Officer (CEO) - it's your choice. I prefer to keep it simple. I'm just a plain old Director. That's what's on my business card.

Setting up with an Umbrella Company

This is really very easy to do. You're doing this because you don't want the hassle of running your own business and all that goes with it. Umbrella companies do invoicing, credit control, book-keeping, record keeping, process your expenses and deal with your tax and NI contributions. Often, they will include Professional Indemnity Insurance, Public Liability Insurance and Employers Liability Insurance. It's a great option if you want to take the easy route.

When you join an umbrella company, you become an employee of theirs. So, you get all the rights of an employee. You get paid holidays (they keep some cash back from you to allow for this) and you can claim statutory sick pay (after 4 days consecutive absence). They will quite often help you when your contract ends – after all, it's within their interests to get you on to another role in order for them to continue earning their fees.

VAT is chargeable by the umbrella company for their services and you still charge VAT to your clients (assuming you're over the threshold). You work inside what is called 'IR35' – that is you are an employee and you pay tax in the normal way.

Obviously, umbrella companies charge a fee for their services. You have to be really careful when selecting an umbrella company, that you are clear what services they are providing and even clearer about what is not provided and what they may charge in addition to their standard fee. Remember, the only thing that differs between them is their fee and their service levels. It doesn't matter which company you choose, you still pay the same amount of statutory tax that is due. Expect to pay anywhere between £40 and £200 per month. An average cost would be about £100 per month.

The main steps to selecting an umbrella company are;

1. Be clear about what you want from your umbrella company. Some things to think about are:

    a. A fair price for the service

    b. They are a good sized company and have a lot of clients

    c. They offer insurances to cover you

    d. They pay you quickly

    e. They have enough staff to be able to answer your questions or you get a named point contact

    f. You can access them when you need (i.e. not just 9am to 5pm)

    g. You know what you have to do to get out of the contract

2. Ring up a selection of umbrella companies (see Top 10 questions below). You will need your hourly/daily rate, the start and end dates of your contract, how you intend to travel to your client each day (train, tube, car etc) and what you expect to spend on food and drink each day (they will allow daily expenses)

10 questions to ask when selecting an Umbrella Company
1.   What services do you offer?
2.   How many people use your service?
3.   How many people are there in your company? How long have you been in business?
4.   How much do you charge for these services? How is the charge applied?
5.   What extras do I have to pay for? Is there a set up fee?
6.   How do people access your services on a daily basis?
7.   Can you confirm that I will be their employee with full employee rights?
8.   How often do you run your payroll (daily, weekly or monthly)? If weekly or monthly, when do I need to get my timesheet in? How often do I get paid?
9.   What insurances are included in the price?
10. What are the exit clauses to get out of the contract?

Here's some checks to make as you're making your selection:

Check if the umbrella company charges a fixed fee – that way, if your day rate goes up, you still get charged the same amount.

Check out how much they charge for same day (CHAPs) payments – some absorb the cost, others can charge up to £20 per transaction.

Check if you have your own dedicated account manager – this is really useful and you can build up more of a personal relationship with them and they get to know you and what kind of contract you're on etc.

Check if there are additional charges for processing expenses – some do charge some don't.

Check out which insurances are covered in the fee by the umbrella company – the mandatory insurances are Employers Liability and Public Liability insurance (but just check!). The majority of umbrella companies also include Professional Indemnity Insurance (PII), which covers you against the legal costs and claims for compensation if you make a mistake or are found to be negligent.

Check if the umbrella company offers a stakeholder pension scheme – if they do, then you can take advantage of this and make most use of your tax allowances. The amount of tax relief can be as much as 48% - so for every £100 invested, you only pay £52 and the tax man pays the rest. By doing this, you avoid paying income tax, employers and employees NI contributions.

Check if you still pay their administration fee even when you're not working – it is common NOT to charge if you're not working.

Check what expenses you can claim – you can claim travel expenses to and from your client. This is because your permanent place of work is deemed to be your home address and the client is your temporary work place.

3.   Decide which umbrella company you want and sign up with them.

Most umbrella companies will sign you up inside 24 hours (before you can change your mind!). This can involve you signing up to a contract of employment with them. You'll need to provide bank details, NI number and forward your P45 if you have one.

Once you have your contract sorted, you provide all the necessary details to them like start and end date, client and agency details and the hourly or daily rate. You also need to provide the agency with your umbrella company details. The agency or the client will forward a copy of the contract for the umbrella company to sign – this is because the contract is between the client (or the agency) and your employer – the umbrella company.

After you have completed your first period of chargeable time with the client (sometimes a week, but more often a month), the umbrella company will invoice the client and receive payment. The umbrella company will then deduct tax and NI and their fees and pay you within their agree timeframe –sometime this can be a week, a few days or even the same day (but watch out for them charging more for this same day service).

Setting up with Reduced-Tax/'Offshore' Company

Right, this section is for the adventurous amongst you, or put another way, the 'off-the-scale' risk people. You are the kind of person who is saying "I'm going contracting and I'm going to make as much money as possible out of it". If you're completely fine with taking risks, then this could be for you. The rewards can be quite a lot higher. You can get a reduced tax scheme where you pay almost no tax. I wouldn't go with them, I've heard of them, I've never pursued them and I wouldn't do it. However, there are other schemes, mostly based offshore – being Europe, Isle-of-Man, Channel Islands etc – that do offer good rewards and their schemes have been checked out by the HMRC and usually a very good barrister or QC. These are worth looking at. There are different ways that they approach the way they remunerate you but it can include paying you a basic salary – just enough to keep you below the tax threshold – and paying you the rest via a Loan, which you don't then repay.

OK, so now you're worried. A loan you don't repay? That's not right, is it? And many people agree but there is a way through this that allows you to get paid 80% - 85% of your invoiced amount. Ah, so now you're back with me? Yes, it's true, you can pay 15% - 20% tax through these schemes and they have been checked by the HMRC and QC and they are legitimate. The way it works is really simple. You record your time, submit a timesheet, the 'payment services company' then suggests a payment to a Loan company for all the good work you've done and they pay you once they have received payment form the client – subject to the usual settlement period (often 30 days). And you get a payment, as a salary and another payment as a loan. There are literally thousands of contractors getting paid in this way. It is not a small business. You sign a contract of employment with the offshore company and you are classed as an employee. So you will pay tax through PAYE and National Insurance but only on the relatively small salary component of your payment.

What's the catch? Well, if you don't like risk, don't touch this with a barge pole. There is a chance that legislation will change and may mean you become liable for taxes and the HMRC is getting very good at back dating taxes, which would be a problem. The 'reduced tax' schemes are under very close scrutiny by the HMRC especially as more and more contractors venture down this route. It's a balance. You have to weigh up the rewards versus the risk. Only you can call it.

You are getting into the blurred lines that exist between tax evasion and tax avoidance. Tax evasion is illegal and includes dishonest tax reporting and deliberately misrepresenting the true state of the tax that you owe. Tax avoidance is the legal use of tax laws to reduce your tax burden. One mans avoidance is another man's (HMRC's) evasion!

Other complications arise from the fact that some client companies will absolutely not deal with 'payment services' companies, especially if they are based offshore. There is a way round this where the payment services company has an onshore UK presence and some client companies are ok with this. They don't like dealing with offshore companies because they perceive a risk that they could become liable for any tax due if for some reason you don't pay it. Getting the payment channel right in these circumstances can be time consuming and often doesn't work in the first month!

So, if you're not put off the whole idea already, then here are some questions to pose to any potential offshore payments services company:

10 questions to ask when selecting an Offshore Payments Services Company
1. Has the scheme been reviewed by a leading tax counsel and approved by HMRC?
2. What services do you offer?
3. How many contractors use your service?
4. How many people are there in your company? How long have you been in business?
5. How much do you charge for these services? How is the charge applied?
6. What extras do I have to pay for? Is there a set up fee?
7. Is there a minimum contract, 'lock-in' or notice period?
8. How often do you run your payroll (daily, weekly or monthly)? If weekly or monthly, when do I need to get my timesheet in? How often do I get paid?
9. What insurances are included in the price?
10. What are the exit clauses to get out of the contract?

I would only recommend you go for this type of scheme once you've become accustomed to contracting. It is not for the faint hearted but you will potentially get fed up with paying so much tax – corporation tax, personal tax, tax on dividends – that this might seem to be a valid option. Do your research carefully.

This might make you think twice

- HMRC has been allocated £994m up to 2015 to reinvest in the fight against tax avoidance, evasion and fraud
- They expect to reclaim up to £1 billion through recent agreement with the Isle of Man, Guernsey and Jersey
- The level of penalty on tax evaded offshore is 200%
- A recent court ruling judged that is was permissible for the HMRC to claim back tax underpayments retrospectively.

Ensure you do your due diligence on your reduced tax scheme company. And remember the golden rule – if it sounds too good to be true, it probably is too good to be true!

Start Up Costs

You might wonder how much it's going to cost you to set up as a contractor and the beauty is that it's probably less than you think. It does depend which kind of business you are getting into of course. If you're going to be a contract photographer, then clearly you're going to need camera kit. What I will outline here is the situation for the vast majority of contractors, who are going into a company to be a resource.

Company Set Up – there are 3 options here; deal with Companies House yourself, use an agent to do this or use an accountant. You should budget for £30 - £150 depending on which option you choose.

Web Site set up – again, you can choose to do this yourself or get someone to do it for you. Website set up should cost almost nothing if you do it yourself but can get pricey when using others and you could need from £250 - £1,000 to get this sorted depending on how sophisticated you want your site to be. Ongoing costs range from £0 to £30/month, again depending on what services you need.

Laptop – this is the question I get asked all the time – "Should I buy a laptop?" The simple answer is yes you should. The reason is simple. There is nothing better than turning up on client site on the first day, to find out that "IT haven't quite sorted your computer access yet!" for you to be able to flip out your laptop and be able to produce work on that for the first few days – even if it's writing a set of roles and responsibilities or a set of deliverables or a job list. It just looks great.

Equally, it's useful as a distinction to draw between your work and your business/personal emails. Do be careful though. Some clients don't like or even forbid personal laptops on site and if they do, just be careful about how often you're seen on your laptop doing your business work. Lunchtime is ok, after hours is ok.

Don't go mad and get the latest all singing, high-performance machine. Top of my list is weight – it has to be light to be able to carry round in a backpack along with all my notes etc. Don't go too small either. You need to be able to have a good enough screen to be able to do presentations and documents without squinting. I would allow around £1,000.

Phone – quite simply, get the best you can get hold of. Smartphones are brilliant for not just calls but keeping all your contacts, accessing your emails, keeping track of your bank accounts etc. The best thing on my iPhone – Train Times app, which tells me the platform my train is leaving from ahead of the screens in the main hall at Paddington and gets me on the train about 1 minute before anyone else (who doesn't have the app!) so I get a seat and get settled in before the onslaught. This is closely followed by Google Maps, which has got me to clients (and evening venues) quickly and efficiently on innumerable occasions.

Try to get on a good deal. Work out what you are likely to need. Unlimited texts and calls are fairly standard for business users but watch out for data limits. Unlimited data can be expensive and not really required. I would advise at least 1GB per month on your phone will suffice. You should allow around £50/month for a fully kitted out phone.

Business Cards – do get business cards but don't spend a fortune on them. There are genuinely fewer and fewer occasions where business cards are needed these days. But it's always a nice touch. This is an outward/client/world facing piece of your brand, so do ensure it looks professional. You can do your own with a little effort. Allow £100.

Business Stationery – if you can create your own logo and cards, then you can do your own stationery. I had some made up but it's easier to just produce this electronically now. Allow £100.

Business Attire – this is worth investing in. Be careful if you are getting into made-to-measure suits though. Some clients may have a problem if you're being seen to be spending a lot on suits if they're not.

Trade Body Subscriptions – depending on your line of business, you may need to join a trade body in order to carry out your work. These vary considerably so check carefully. Most people will not need to belong to a trade body in general contracting.

Business Insurance – you will need to get yourself insured (as mentioned previously). The 3 types of insurance are Public Liability, Employee Liability and Professional Indemnity insurance. It is common to find insurance companies that will cover all three in one policy. Shop around though. The costs vary widely. Allow £250 per year.

Travel Case – if you work away from home, getting a decent travel case is essential. Roller cases save your back – get one with two wheels not four – they work great in the shop but lousy in the real world. Equally, check out the noise they make on pavements. Noisy wheels are an embarrassment! Get a good one and make sure you buy one that will fit in an aircraft overhead locker so you can carry on your luggage and not have to wait at the other end. Saves time and hassle. A good case will cost around £100.

Car – depending on how much travelling you have to do on the road will determine the kind of car you need. In my early days of consulting, I had a choice of a number of cars in the car pool. Of course, I went for the GTi, why wouldn't you, until you find yourself on a motorway, in the summer, in a noisy car, with no air conditioning, with the windows down to keep cool and the stereo on full volume to be able to hear the music. I used to end up drenched and deaf by the time I got to the client site!

My advice is get a big comfortable car, definitely air-conditioned, possibly automatic. Make it a diesel to get the fuel economy. Choose a car that's not too flashy. Turning up in a car that's significantly better than the client's car can be tricky.

Office Space – again, this will depend on the type of business you are moving into. If you need a studio to carry out your business or need to meet clients face to face frequently, then an office is essential. Look around carefully and make use of local schemes that initially give office space freely, or at a nominal charge, to start ups. If you do have to pay, the rate is measured in terms of £/square foot (yes, I know it's old fashioned, but that's the way it is!). Cheaper rates are around £15/sqft up to £40/sqft. Figure out how much space you really need and don't take on too much to start with. Best advice is to use the services of an office letting agent and take their advice.

Most contractors will not need an office to operate their business. Instead, most use a room at home which is their focal point if they need to do some work or administration.

IT Kit – memory sticks, data storage – memory sticks are essential as is the ability to be able to back up your data on to a separate hard drive or store virtually using cloud services. A big capacity memory stick will cost around £40. Top tip – sellotape your telephone number onto it – just in case you lose it, like I did once – ouch, that hurt! A large capacity hard drive (1TB) costs around £70 but is unlikely to be the kind of thing you carry around with you.

Be careful about using these on client site. Most clients lock down their USB ports on their computers, so you can get information in but not out. Even doing a 'good deed' of providing your expert presentation and loading that on to client systems, can be frowned upon. Introducing a virus can get you fired!

So a summary of potential start up costs looks like this:

Type of Cost	Minimum Cost	Likely Cost	High Cost
Company Set Up	£30	£50	£150
Website Set Up	£0	£250	£1,000
Laptop	£0	£1,000	£2,000
Phone	£10/month	£40/month	£60/month
Business Cards	£0	£10	£100
Business Stationery	£20	£20	£100
Business Attire	£0	£300	£1,000
Subscriptions	£0	£0	£250
Business Insurance	£200	£200	£600
Travel Case	£0	£100	£200
Car	£0	£0	£300/month
Office Space	£0	£0	£1,000/month
IT Kit	£0	£100	£200
Total	£250 + £10/month	£2,030 + £40/month	£5,600 + £1,360/month

It's a starting point for you. The actual start up costs will very much depend on your own circumstances but I wanted to point out that you can make decisions that mean you can get into contracting for minimal outlay. Most contractors are going to be between columns 1 and 2. My advice would be don't make the cost of start up be a hurdle for you.

The minimum you need is a company name, a phone and insurance, that's it. Next on my list would be a laptop and back up for files but this needn't cost a lot either. Find someone with an older laptop they don't use and borrow it! There's ways round these costs. Once you've submitted your first invoice, things will seem a whole lot rosier!

You and your Business

Once you've set up your business, it's important to think about it as a separate body. Here's why. If you've set up on your own, you are the only person in the business, you do all the hard work to earn the money, submit the invoices, make payments and run the business. So the money that comes in is yours right? No, it isn't. It belongs to your company. So anything to do with spending money on the company is fine to charge to the company but you have to be able to get your money out of the company before you can spend it on yourself. Whichever trading structure you choose, you have to think of the money going into a separate entity called your company. When you have taken all the costs and expenses into account and then the taxes that are or will become due, then you have a right to the remaining money, which you can then 'pay' to yourself.

Once you've got your head around this, then you can see why it's best to separate everything to do with the business from your personal life. So set up a separate bank account for the business. Have a separate credit card and cheque book (if you need one) for the business. Put all business related expenses and costs through that company bank account. Don't start paying your own private expenses through the business.

BUT and it's a big but, this is one of the best parts about running your own business. You can put expenses through the company that are legitimate. So you can put expenses in for your pension, your private health insurance (which you can extend to your family as a company perk), your car (if you use it on business (more on this later), your Personal Indemnity Insurance, your life cover, in fact anything that you would expect to receive through a permanent position in terms of allowances or perks can be charged through your own company. All these expenses have the effect of reducing your net profit but then you pay less tax. There are strict rules around what you can and cannot charge through your company (see later in the section on Tax).

The way I think about it is this. When I walk out of the house on a Monday morning, I'm working for my own company. If I step on a train, I charge it to the company. If I use the tube in London, I charge it. Wherever I stay, I charge it. If I eat a meal in the evening, I charge it. I'm away from home on company business and can reasonably expect the company to pick up the bill (just as you would expect in a normal company).

When I get home and I get in the car to drive my daughter to a swimming lesson, that's my cost. I can't charge it. It's personal and not to do with the business. If I drive to visit my accountant at the weekend, that is company business and I will charge it.

There's more on allowable expenses later in the tax section.

HOW TO RUN AND CONTROL YOUR BUSINESS

There are basically two routes to head down here. Either you do it, or you don't i.e. you get an accountant to do it.

Running your own Company

It's not as hard as you might first think. I am going to focus on you as an individual contractor running your own Company, not setting up a company that employs others because that's where things do get more involved (Tax, NI, Pensions, Benefits, HS&E…you name it!)

Running your own Business Day to Day, Week to Week

In your day-to-day life as a contractor, you set foot outside your front door/office door and, assuming you're on legitimate Business, you are charging to your Company. So it's sensible to keep all charges to the Company separate. I use a credit card in the Company's name to charge in. So all your travel, hotel/accommodation expenses etc (see section on what you can claim later) you can put through as a cost.

KEEP YOUR RECEIPTS

Be religious about this. It helps. Again, you have two choices. You can do your own accounting or you can use an accountant to prepare your accounts. Either way, you need receipts to keep HMRC happy. It's useful to stick them all in an envelope each month and - up to you how you do things – you can either build up your accounts throughout the year (recommended) or leave it to the end of the year and do it in one fell swoop. Or better still, give it all to an accountant to deal with! (see next section on choosing an Accountant).

Week-to-week, you may need to fill in a time sheet to record the number of days you've worked. You will need (usually) to get this signed off by your day-to-day Manager at the Client site and then submit it. Sometimes, agents have their own electronic systems for doing this, sometimes you have to faff about faxing or scanning or sending hard copies in the post – or sometimes all of the above! Sometimes, the client may need you to fill their own timesheet to keep a track of spend, so you can end up spending a reasonable amount of time just doing admin at the end of a week.

Running your own Business Month to Month

On a monthly basis, you will need to invoice the client and pay yourself (assuming you're not doing this weekly).

Monthly Invoicing

This should be very straight forward. Assuming you have an agent in place, you will be submitting your timesheets as described above. Then, once a month, they should invoice the client on your behalf. They will copy you into the correspondence and, quite often, the money rolls into your bank account electronically.....

...up to one month later! Remember that payment terms are usually up to 30days. Some agents offer to put the money into your account after 2 days and this is possible, it's just that they are taking a risk and a cash-flow hit because the client will usually pay the agent between 30-60 days after invoicing – if they're lucky!

So do check the terms of your contract. You get used to being a month in arrears. And you get used to big months (up to 25 working days occasionally – puts a grin on your face!) and the not so big months, like when you've been on holiday. Suddenly you realise how expensive holidays are now – you pay for the holiday AND you lose revenue – bonus!

If you do contract directly with the client or the agent requires it, you will need to submit a monthly invoice. This is not difficult. A typical template needs to be on Company headed paper, have your Company address, the date, the address of the recipient (agent or client), a Purchase Order number (provided by the agent or client), a title of the project or piece of work you're doing and, at most, a three liner detailing fees, expenses (if appropriate) and VAT (if appropriate). You need to sign it as the Company Director and on the footer, you need to have the Company name, address, Company Registration number and VAT number. (See the Resources section on www.breakfreegocontracting.com).

You will need to make sure you know where you need to send your invoice. Often you'll be sending it to Finance and the Accounts Receivables department. In a large organisation, your invoice can get lost or questions can arise especially when you send in your first one. My advice is to 'mother' the first one through, so phone up the finance guys and ensure they've received it and then that they are acting on it. Also check when they are intending to pay you and they're not under some illusion that it's going to be ok to get back to you in 90 days. It happens!

Paying Yourself

There's only one thing better than invoicing the client monthly and looking forward to all that lovely revenue coming in and that's actually paying yourself. It's quite funny the first time - determining how much you want to and can pay yourself, because it is up to you! You need to work out how much and you need to make sure you're not taking too much out of the company that it can't pay its tax bills and other liabilities.

But it is relatively straight forward. I suggest you take advice from an accountant on the latest tax position for your specific situation at the outset. They will likely advise you to pay yourself a salary and an amount in dividends. A dividend is a payment made by a company to you as a shareholder in recognition of the profits the company has made. It is usually a fixed amount per share.

For you, this means that your own company pays you according to your shareholding depending on how much profit you have made. So if you earn £100,000 in a year and your net profit comes out as £60,000, and you're the only shareholder (i.e. you own 100% of the shares), you can pay yourself £60,000 as a dividend, which means that you take all the money out of the company. It is more tax efficient to take your money out of the company as a dividend so you should be aiming to maximise this where you can.

One way of doing this is to pay yourself a dividend as you go through the year, rather than in a lump sum at the end of the year. Each month, as you are paying yourself a minimal salary, you can pay yourself a dividend BUT this assumes that you are pretty confident that you will continue to earn a similar amount for the remainder of the year, so better to be cautious if you do adopt this approach.

However, a simple approach is outlined below:

Assume you're earning £400/day and you know you're going to be on the project for 6 months (so some degree of certainty).

Monthly income	£8,000
Less costs (assume 15%)	£1,200
Less salary	£600
Less allowance for Corporation Tax (20%)	£1,240
Profit for distribution (Dividend)	£4,960

So, in theory you can write a cheque of deposit into your account for £5,560 for this month. Not bad eh? But a more cautious approach might be to leave some money in the company to cover you if you are out of work for a few weeks. It's up to you how much you put aside but suppose at the end of your 6 month contract, you were out of work for 2 weeks, that's £4,000 lost revenue. To cover this, you would need to retain around £650 per month. If you assumed a 4 week gap, you'd need to retain around £1,300 per month. So just pay yourself less in the short term and build a buffer in the company.

Do take into account that by receiving dividend payments that you will be liable for tax at the year end. You should allow between 20% and 37.5% tax on the dividends you pay yourself. As ever, it's not quite that simple, so look in the Appendices to see the way in which dividend tax is calculated.

To make a dividend payment, you should always (says HMRC) hold a Directors' meeting to declare the dividend payment and keep minutes of the meeting, even if you're the only Director. A favourite meeting place is down the pub or at a nice restaurant! You should always create a dividend voucher. On it should be date the company name, names of the shareholders being paid a dividend, amount of the dividend and the amount of the 'dividend tax credit'. To work this out, you divide the dividend amount by 9. So a £900 dividend will create a dividend tax credit of £900/9 = £100, which you add to the dividend amount giving a total dividend amount of £1,000. This is the amount you as a recipient of the dividend will get taxed on. To help you, there is a template on the website – www.breakfreegocontracting.com

It goes without saying that you do not touch any VAT you charge. This belongs to the VAT man. Put it in a separate account and don't touch it until you need to pay it (more in next section).

ALWAYS PAY THE VAT MAN

Equally, you must retain the money for your Corporation Tax. Put it away in a high-interest savings account – if you can find one. My favourite was to buy premium bonds through the year, so at least there was the possibility (however small!) of a windfall. And just to be clear, if you did win, it belongs to the company not you! You would need to take advice on how best to get a lot of money out of the company in a tax efficient way. Nice problem to have! And no I didn't win!

Running your own Business Quarterly

When you set up for VAT registration, you have the option as to when you pay your VAT. My advice would be to do this quarterly. It means you keep on top of things, makes sure you don't spend the VAT money and, if you're on the FRS scheme, it means you get a little bonus more frequently. So, the kindly folk at HMRC will send you a reminder that you need to pay your VAT. You can fill in a form or, a lot more easily, do it all on line at:

http://www.hmrc.gov.uk/vat/vat-online/index.htm

You have to work out the amount you have earned (invoiced), any input VAT (not required if you're on FRS) and the level of VAT you've charged. You then submit a payment for the amount that you owe. Simple as that.

Running your own Business Annually

On an annual basis, you will need to create and submit your accounts to Companies House, complete a Company Tax Return and send it to HMRC, pay Corporation Tax and complete an annual return for Companies House.

The timelines for these are:

Action	Deadline
File annual accounts with Companies House	9 months after your company's financial year ends
File a Company Tax Return	12 months after your company's financial year ends
Pay Corporation Tax	9 months and 1 day after your company's financial year ends
Submit an Annual Statement to Companies House	28 days before the anniversary of your Companies incorporation

If you miss these deadlines, you can be fined. So don't!

Creating and submitting your accounts, paying Corporation Tax and filing a tax return, as we've mentioned before, is either going to be you or your accountant. I choose the services of an accountant to do this but keep my expenses records all together, provide him with the bank statements and cheque books/paying-in books, dividend payments and dividend vouchers and he does the rest. Remember, you are still liable as a Director of your company for your accounts. You have to sign the accounts before they are sent. So if your accountant makes a mess of the return, it's your problem not theirs! The accounts should be very straight forward and amount to only a few pages – a Profit and Loss statement and a Balance Sheet, with any suitable notes.

Each year, Companies House will write to you to remind you to submit your annual statement about your company. It's just checking you haven't moved, who the Directors are and their latest shareholding. You do this online at:

https://ewf.companieshouse.gov.uk//seclogin?tc=1

You will need to register in order to get a password and an authentication code, which is specific to your company. You need to do this in the 28 days leading up to the anniversary of the incorporation of your company. It costs £13 and takes only a few minutes to complete, once you have it set up. If you don't do it, you can get fined and Companies House can dissolve your company and stop it trading – so do keep on top of this.

Do remember that the first time you do register, Companies House will ask you which sector you are operating in or the SIC (Standard Industry Classification) code for your business. It is important to get this right. Refer to the chapter Setting yourself up in Self-Employment – deciding on a name for your business and the chapter on VAT – Flat

Rate VAT scheme so you can work out the right SIC code for your business.

Getting an Accountant to Run your Business

So, do you get one or not? There are definitely pros and cons to this.

10 pros and cons of using an accountant
1. They stay on top of the latest tax situations
2. They can help you plan for future tax liabilities
3. They can fill in and file your tax returns on your behalf
4. They can come up with ideas about how to grow your company
5. They can provide access to their own network who may be able to help
6. You can lose control of your business affairs
7. They can cost a lot of money
8. They sometimes don't spend enough time looking after your account
9. They are definitely variable in the quality of service that they offer
10. They are not liable for the accuracy of your tax return – you are!

The biggest pro is about the amount of time it saves you. You're now in the mindset of every hour you put into something it is costing you money versus something else you could be doing. You are your own boss now and it's important to focus on the important things. So if you spend a couple of days a month doing the books, then you're not necessarily earning fees or building your network or prospecting for new work. Is this a good use of your time? For some it may be. If you're already a qualified accountant or have a close family member who is, then why not do your own books. And there are plenty of easy to use (or so they say) packages on the market and not very much money. So it is tempting to do it and get to understand everything in the tax and accounting world, after all, a simple business model where you're the only worker or one of a few is relatively easy to keep on top of.

I would always advise using an accountant. A good one should pay for themselves each year in the advice that they can give to you, that saves you the money you spend on them. True, there aren't many loopholes as a contractor but they should be aware of them. An acid test question for them is FRS – Flat-Rate VAT scheme (see the chapter on VAT). Most contractors earning over the VAT threshold can benefit from this. If your accountant looks at you blankly when you mention this, walk out and go find someone else.

10 things to ask your potential Accountant
1. How many of your current active clients are contractors?
2. What size of company do you normally deal with?
3. How many of your accountants are fully qualified and who deals with what?
4. Who will look after me? Will it be the same person through the year?
5. How is your accounting business doing (e.g. thriving and expanding)?
6. What are your fees and how and when do you charge them (monthly/annually)?
7. What would your accountancy firm do each year to ensure you pay for yourself?
8. What information do you need from me monthly/quarterly/annually?
9. How will you communicate with me (email/phone/meetings) and how often?
10. Why should I choose you over all the other accountants?

Here's a little bit of explanation about these questions:

1. You need to know if they are used to dealing with one-man bands and in particular contractors.

2. If they generally mainly deal with larger companies, this can be a problem. The best situation is where the accountants have a good spread across a range of sizes of company – some of the tricks of the trade that larger companies are able to play might be applicable to smaller ones.

3. It's important to know if there are a number of qualified accountants and what heir spread is. They may very well have 5 qualified accountants but if they major on foreign companies or

specialist pension arrangements, then that's not much use to you. You need to know that you have at least one qualified accountant who deals specifically with smaller companies

4. You need to know who is going to be nominated to look after you. If all your initial dealings with the accountants are focused through the lead partner, but they are not going to be the ones who take care of you, then you need to meet he person who is to work out if you're going to get on with them. Equally, you need to establish if the nominated person is going to be constant throughout the year – i.e. that they are not planning to change your point of contact.

5. You need to know that their business is successful and conversely that they're not going to be out of business in the next year. Find out what their plans are for the future and if expanding their contractor base is a part of their vision.

6. Fees can be charged monthly, quarterly or annually. Whichever way, you need to know in order to plan in for the costs. You also need to know the level of the fees and how they are applied. If they cover off the company accounts, can they also cover off your personal tax return? And is this included in the fees? You need to know what happens if they have to deal with any queries raised by HMRC – is this covered? And what charges may arise above their basic fee.

7. Most good accountants should be spending sufficient time on your account to generate savings to you that pay for their own fee. This is where working with a larger firm may not be a great idea as the effort they put in is often proportionate to the size of the fees they are likely to bring in. They will generally focus on larger companies.

8. You need to know what you have to do to ensure you deliver what the accountants need. At one extreme is providing them with a bag of receipts and letting them sort it all out, at the other, monthly submissions, all neatly labelled and summarised. Get to know how

much work you are expected to do – this might explain the level of fees so make sure you're comparing accountants' services fairly.

9. Find out how you will interact with each other. Face to face meetings are great unless you're meeting during the week when you could be earning fees. Do they work at weekends or see their clients in the evenings?

10. Your accountants should know who their competitors are – they are in demand but all keen to win new business. They should have a clear idea about why they are the best solution for you.

The main point is to find an accountant that you can get on with and one that is going to look after you. If they answer the questions above well, you probably won't go far wrong. Do take people's personal recommendations into account when you're selecting your accountant but at the end of the day, you have to be comfortable that they will look after your interests and you need to make that decision.

How much you should pay for your accountants' services is a tricky question to answer absolutely. I know some contractors who pay barely £100 per year. I pay around £1,000 per year but this includes doing the accounts for both my limited companies and my personal tax return. I do a fair amount of work, summarising my receipts and providing copies of all my dividend paperwork and all my bank statements. I put it in a big A4 file and send it off each year.

WHAT YOU CAN CHARGE TO YOUR BUSINESS

It's important you get this right or you will have the tax man battering down your door. It is relatively simple. The golden rule is that the expense must be 'wholly, exclusively and necessarily incurred in the performance of your day to day business'. If you apply this rule, then you won't go far wrong but there are some expenses that you might think satisfy this criteria but don't – classics are client entertainment and business attire, neither of which may be claimed via your company.

The simplest way of claiming expenses is to get your accountant to work it out. If you are regularly incurring expenses by living away from home (e.g. hotels, meals etc) then it can be sensible to know what is allowable and claim these back from your company on a regular basis.

Expense Type	Claimable?	Comments
Salaries	Yes	Use up your personal allowance and that or your spouse or partner if they work for the company
Pension	Yes	You need to have an Employer's Contribution Scheme (see later)
Living Accommodation/ Rental fees	Yes	If you have to stay away from home because it takes too long to get home each night, then this is chargeable including utilities and Council Tax

Expense Type	Claimable?	Comments
Mileage	Yes	Better to claim mileage this way than buying a company car. Currently, you can claim 45p per mile for the first 10,000 miles and 25p per mile thereafter. Motor bikes - 24p per mile Cycles – 20p per mile
Training and Development	Yes	Yes, but only to maintain your skills, not t acquire a new skill
Stationery	Yes	…including couriers
Computer Equipment	Yes	…including software
Personal Incidental Expenses	Yes	…when staying away from home, to the tune of £5 per night in the UK and £10 per night abroad! Woohoo! Don't spend it all at once.
Books and Magazines	Yes	As long as they are associated with your business
Advertising	Yes	
Companies House Fees	Yes	
Bank Charges and Interest	Yes	
Professional Subscriptions	Yes	
Legal and Professional Fees	Yes	

Expense Type	Claimable?	Comments
Leasing costs	Yes	
Insurances	Yes	
Company Formation Fees	Yes	
Postage	Yes	
Telephone, Mobile and Broadband	Yes but…	Yes, but only the proportion of the bill that is for business – all your personal calls should not be charged and yes, this means going through your bill line by line!
Hotel and Accommodation	Yes but…	Yes, but any nights away for pleasure cannot be charged
Bus, Train and Taxis	Yes but…	As long as they are incurred wholly… etc
Subsistence – eating	Yes but…	Meals (Breakfast, Dinner) as part of an overnight stay, yes. Or because you have to leave very early or stay very late. Lunch – not really – you have to eat in any case!
Business Gifts	Yes but…	Only gifts with your corporate branding on and costing less than £50 is allowable
Childcare Costs	Yes but…	Yes, only via the Government's Childcare Voucher scheme up to £55 per week – see terms and conditions

Expense Type	Claimable?	Comments
Home Working expenses	Yes but...	Yes, but this is a tricky area and depends on your circumstances – look at the HMRC website at: www.hmrc.gov.uk/incometax/relief-household You can claim up to £4 per week without additional supporting information.
Clothing	No but...	Only protective clothing
Entertainment (for yourself or clients)	No	You as an individual can claim the money back from your company but you can't claim tax relief
Gym Membership	No	
Prescriptions	No	
Weekly Food Shop	No	
Private School Fees	No	...nice try!
Nursing Home Payments	No	

This list is a guide and you should check the latest allowances through the HMRC website. Do seek guidance from an accountant to make sure.

Claiming Travel Expenses

This should be easy right? If you use your own car or motorbike for your business, you can and should claim money off your company – and make a little bit of a personal profit in the process. The reason that this subject warrants a separate section is that there are some complex rules around it. So here goes.

For most contractors, travelling between home and a client site will constitute a chargeable business journey. The place of work you go to is viewed by HMRC as temporary and your home is often your business address. If you operate from an office, then that is classed as your business address. You can charge the whole journey to the client site. Up to a point…

If you spend less than 40% of your normal working time (which, unhelpfully, HMRC don't define!) at your client site, then HMRC deem this as a temporary workplace and all travel expenses are chargeable

If you spend more than 40% of your time on a client site, then you can claim travel expenses as long you don't exceed 24 months. If your travel to the client site is likely to last more than 24 months, then at the point at which you become aware of this, you cannot charge for travel to the client site, because it is deemed to be a permanent place of work. So, if you have a 12 month contract you can charge but if that contract gets extended by 12 months, then you cannot charge for the second 12 months because you 'became aware' of being on site for 24 months after only 12 months. Great! So guess what? You get the client to extend the contract by one day short of 12 months and you're fine!

What you can claim is:

-    Mileage, fares, parking, tolls and taxis AND
-    All necessary food and drink costs incurred during the travel plus

- Any accommodation costs
- Certain meals purchased whilst away from home

The costs must be incurred because of the business travel. So, in theory, as soon as you walk out of the door until you come back home, all of the above are chargeable. You can travel first class if you wish, as long as the company can afford it, but the HMRC do frown on anything that looks like excess. So, just be sensible. After all, it is still your company money that you are spending.

To make your claim from HMRC, you have two choices

a. To claim actual expenses incurred, where you have to provide receipts
b. To use flat rate expense claims, called "scale-rates", where you don't have to supply receipts and are a Director of you own company.

a. Using this method, you must keep all receipts and keep all records of mileages. You can then make a claim against your company and, at year end, you would submit the expense summary (P11D) as part of your tax form into HMRC and they take it into account as part of your overall tax position.

b. Using this method, there are no receipts to keep and expenses claimed are not subject to Tax or National Insurance! So far, so good.

You must get an agreement in place with HMRC ahead of the tax year in which you want to start using this method.
However, the rates are not too great:

Breakfast – can be claimed for early starters (before 6am) max £5.00

Daily One Meal Rate – where you've been away for more than 5 hours   max £5.00

Daily Two Meal Rate – where you've been away for more than 10 hours   max £10.00

Late Evening Meal Rate – for irregular finishes beyond 8pm max £15.00
(this is claimable in addition to the rates above)

Overnight Expenses Rate – for things like newspapers, laundry max £5.00

You can claim the actual cost incurred if you wish. You should keep records of what meals have been claimed for. Overseas rates apply differently and you should check the latest via HMRC.

You can, however, pick and choose between the two methods throughout the year, for each expense – best of luck with this one!

My advice is to roughly work out which scheme is likely to work out better for you, then try it out (make sure you agree the scale rate with the HMRC ahead of the tax year). If you end up not benefitting as much as you thought, then modify your approach and let HMRC know. Me, I claim actual expense. I do keep every receipt. It can be a pain but you know exactly where you're at.

VAT

Value Added Tax (or VAT) is a tax applied to goods or services in relation to the value added to that service or good by the company. VAT is applied to many (but not all) standard rated goods and services, from raw materials right the way through to the end consumer. Everyone along the way can offset the amount of VAT they charge to their customers by the amount of VAT they pay on their materials that they need to produce the good or service. Only the consumer at the end of the chain cannot reclaim against VAT. They just pay the tax on the good or service they receive and that's it. So the Government finally claims VAT off all consumers in the end.

How this works for contractors is relatively simple, you'll be pleased to hear. A contractor is nothing much more than you, what you know, a computer or laptop and a bunch of output that you produce for a client. Our business model is very simple. We don't really have goods coming in (like raw materials) that we then convert and add value to. In fact, for most contractors, when they charge VAT, they will recover it and not really offset any charges against it and then pay it (usually quarterly) back to the Government – HM Revenue and Customs (HMRC).

There is a threshold or limit on the amount of sales you need to achieve before you start charging VAT. Currently (2013), this limit is £79,000. If you do not think you will reach this amount of sales during a year, then you will not charge VAT (currently at 20%) on your invoice.

There is a bit of kudos by having a VAT number. It implies that you are running a company of at least £79,000 turnover for a start which can give clients an element of confidence. Be aware that education and training are VAT-exempt services, so if you are thinking about a business in this area, you won't need to worry about VAT. The best thing to do is to check with HMRC. They have a very good website on this but phone them to make sure about your position.

Assuming you are going to be charging VAT, you will simply charge your client (usually at the end of a month) the number of days multiplied by your day rate, add on any expenses and then add on an extra line for the VAT you are collecting from them. The VAT you reclaim IS NOT YOURS. First, it belongs to the company and second, because you have very little or nothing to offset the charge against, you ARE going to pay it directly back to the VAT man.

A quick rule here is

ALWAYS PAY THE VAT MAN.

(I know, I've mentioned this before, but it is so important!). It can climb to a fair amount of money depending on your rate and when you pay your VAT bill. My advice is to keep it in a separate account, earning a bit of interest but do NOT spend it. It isn't yours!

Flat-Rate VAT Scheme

I'm about to make you buying this book really worth your while. There is a little known scheme run by the HMRC called the Flat-Rate VAT Scheme (or FRS). Under this scheme, you agree to pay a flat fee back to the HMRC, based on your turnover and which industry you are operating within. It takes a lot of work out of retaining and recording VAT against individual sales and purchases. For someone on £400/day, this can amount to a saving of around £250/month!

Because contractors have little or no input VAT (i.e. there are no real incoming charges), you can benefit from less effort and actually make a little money out of VAT! How exciting is that!! The FRS currently only applies to businesses that turnover less than £150,000 per year (excluding VAT), but that equates to a day rate of £700 - 750/day depending on how many days you work. So, it's going to apply to a lot of readers of this book. Also, once you've joined, you can stay in the scheme unless your turnover goes above £230,000. You have to apply to join the FRS and you must be registered for VAT and there are other conditions, so go to the HMRC web site to check out the latest.

This is how it works. You apply the flat rate VAT to all the turnover that you receive INCLUDING the VAT that you charge. Currently, the FRS applicable to typical contractors are:

Category of Business*	Appropriate percentage*	Closest equivalent SIC Code**	SIC Code description
Computer and IT Consultancy or data processing	14.5%	62020	Information Technology consultancy activities
Management Consultancy	14%	70229	Management consultancy activities other than financial management
Business services not listed elsewhere	12%	82990	Other business support service activities

From HMRC VAT website:

http://www.hmrc.gov.uk/vat/start/schemes/flat-rate.htm#4

** from Companies House website:

http://www.companieshouse.gov.uk/about/sic2007.shtml

(There's a full table listing all business activities on the HMRC's VAT website)

So, you will charge a client 20% and the VAT-man will let you re-pay the VAT under this scheme at between 12% and 14.5%!

Perhaps an example will help:

Jo charges £400/day and works for 20 days in a month. She invoices £8,000 and adds on 20% for VAT (assuming no expenses), so the total invoice is for £9,600, which she duly receives into her company bank account 30-days later.

When it comes to paying the VAT-man under the FRS , assuming no other invoices in the period, then Jo will pay VAT back at let's say 14% (as a Management Consultant) on the total amount INCLUDING VAT, which amounts to £1,344 (£9,600 x 14/100).

In summary, Jo charged the client £1,600 VAT and paid back £1,344 VAT, making a tidy little £256 for the month. Multiply this up by 3 invoices a quarter and I reckon this book is worth the cover price for this advice alone!!

PS - amazing how many accountants don't know about the Flat-Rate VAT scheme!

And that's not all. If you are in your first year of VAT, you get a further 1% reduction in the flat-rate amount that is applied, so you could end up paying VAT back for a whole year at 11% and charging the client 20%. I'll drink to that!

Check out the latest at www.hmrc.gov.uk/vat/schemes/flat-rate

...hidden away a bit don't you think.

So, when registering your company, it is important that you put the most appropriate business sector that applies to you because you can benefit from this scheme.

INSURANCES

If you are using a limited company to conduct your business, you will need to consider two types of insurance. These are Company insurance – covering professional indemnity and 'business insurance' – and 'Other' insurances.

Professional Indemnity Insurance (PII)

This insurance covers you in case you make an error when delivering services to a client. When working as a contractor through your own limited company, your company is liable if you make a mistake or an error. You as a Director of that company may become a target for the client if they perceive that they could sue you to recover some or all of their costs. Usually, it has to be a pretty catastrophic impact on the client before they will take action.

So this insurance is designed to cater for a situation when a client decides to take action over an error or even a perceived error. It provides for fees and a possible payout to a client if you have been proved to be professionally negligent.

Small chance – yes, you're right. But unfortunately, you're not likely to be able to get away without having this insurance because most agents will want evidence that you have this insurance in place – otherwise they can get caught in the cross-fire!

You should look around for the best deal because policies do vary and so do premiums! (see website)

If you go through an umbrella company, they will usually have a PII policy in place that will cover you, so you won't need to have PII yourself in this instance.

'Business Insurance'

Business Insurance covers a number of insurances for contractors that can include:

- Public Liability insurance
  This is where any third party makes a claim against your company
- Employers Liability Insurance
  You have to have this – it's a legal requirement - if you have any employees, even if it's you and your other half
- Legal Expenses insurance
  Covers actions or investigations by our chums at HMRC
- Buildings Insurance
  Covers your business premises if you have them
- Business Interruption
  Compensates you loss of earnings in the event of a fire of flood at your place of work
- Portable Equipment insurance
  Sometimes this overall insurance can cover for damage to equipment owned by your business

So again you will need this insurance (agents particularly want the Public Liability insurance). And you will do well to shop around for this too.

Some insurance companies bundle these insurances together and allow you to choose the level of cover you need. It does depend on your individual circumstances so do take advice from your insurers.

For my situation, I'm covered for £1m Professional Indemnity, £2m Public Liability and £10m Employers Liability, with an excess of £500, £250 and nil respectively. You shouldn't be paying more than a couple of hundred pounds for this level of cover.

Other Insurances

As a contractor, you are not covered if you are off work, if you have an illness diagnosed that will keep you off work and you're not covered if you die. So it's worth putting some thought into what cover you want to put in place.

Personal Health Insurance

This covers you in the case where you are not able to work temporarily. You can cover up to 75% of your income and you can have cover start on your first day of absence or defer it for a number of weeks or months. Naturally, the choices you make will be reflected in the premium you pay, so do weigh up the options carefully.

Critical Illness Cover

This covers you in case you contract a critical illness, as defined in the policy – so do read the policy carefully. Typically these insurances pay out a lump sum when you are first diagnosed with the critical illness.

Again, you should consider you own situation carefully and shop around as premium do vary widely.

Life Cover/Death-in-Service Cover

As a permie, you're likely to have this as a benefit, sometimes covering up to 3 or 4 times your salary. Often, if you have a mortgage, you will have life cover in place but it's worth checking out.

All of these insurances can be paid for by your company – you don't have to stump up the premiums personally, however, HMRC will see this as a benefit in kind, so you will get taxed on it! And do seek advice from an Independent Financial Adviser so that you are adequately covered. You don't have to take it all, but do take the time to investigate this. You do feel quite good when it's in place.

UNDERSTANDING CONTRACTOR LEGISLATION

There are a few regulations that are specifically aimed at contractors. The key ones are summarised below. I would suggest taking professional advice if you need to know more about employment law or the latest situation on tax for example. But if you have an understanding of the key points, you can at least know what might impact you.

IR35

There are books written about this subject, mainly by accountants and tax advisers who want your money. Simply, this is about whether, as a contractor, you are deemed by HMRC to be self-employed or not and they have various conditions for evaluating self-employment. They are looking for contractors who are using limited companies and receiving all the tax breaks that this offers but who aren't really taking on any of the risks associated with running a limited company.

In some instances, HMRC are trying to catch out people who have left employment and re-contracted with the same company to provide the same services and thus enjoy a reduced tax regime through a limited company or personal services company.

IR35 only applies to contractors who work via a limited company. If you work via an umbrella company, you pay full tax and NI contributions, so you are outside IR35. If you are a sole trader, then you pay tax and national insurance on your profits and again you are outside IR35. If you use an offshore company, you should check with them about your employment status because in some schemes, you are deemed to be an employee and would therefore be outside IR35.

Bottom line is that if you are caught inside IR35, you will pay more tax and National Insurance, to the tune of about 20% more than if you are outside IR35 and you may receive penalties. The penalties are 30% of unpaid tax if HMRC thinks you've been careless, 70% if they think it's been deliberate, and 100% of unpaid tax if they think you deliberately tried to conceal it!

So, it's quite important. If you get investigated, then it is up to you to convince HMRC that you are self-employed and not 'deemed' employed. However, this is an area that has been notoriously difficult for HMRC to prove and to enforce fines on contractors. The original legislation was poorly conceived and rushed through. Over the years, HMRC has invented more and more complex ways of trying to determine whether contractors are 'disguised' employees. One such, at the time of writing, is the Business Entity Test (see below).

No.	Question	Score
1.	Business Premises Test - Does your business own/rent separate business premises which are separate from your home and client premises?	Yes = 10
2.	PII Test - Do you need professional indemnity insurance?	Yes = 2
3.	Efficiency Test – has your business had the opportunity in the last 24 months to increase your income by working more efficiently e.g. by finishing the work/project earlier than projected but still receiving the full payment?	Yes = 10

No.	Question	Score
4.	Assistance Test – does your business engage one or more workers who generate at least 25% of your business turnover annually?	Yes = 35
5.	Previous PAYE Test – Have you been engaged on PAYE employment terms by your current client/end user within the last financial year with no significant changes to your working arrangements?	Yes = -15 (yes, minus)
6.	Advertising Test – has your business invested over £1,200 on advertising excluding entertainment in the last 12 months?	Yes = 1
7.	Business Plan Test = does your business have a business plan with cash flow forecast that is regularly updated and a business bank account that is separate from your personal account and identified as a business bank account by the bank?	Yes = 1
8.	Repair at own Expense Test – would your business have to bear the cost of having to rectify any mistakes?	Yes = 4
9.	Client Risk Test – has your business been unable to recover payment for work done during the last 24 months in excess of 10% of annual turnover?	Yes = 10
10.	Billing Test – do you invoice for work carried out prior to being paid and negotiate payment terms?	Yes = 2

No.	Question	Score
11.	Personal Service Test – Does your business have the right to send a substitute?	Yes = 2
12.	Substitution Test – has your business hired anyone in the last 24 months to do the contracted work you have taken on?	Yes = 20

High Risk = 0 – 10 points, Medium Risk = 11 – 20 points, Low Risk = 21 points and above

I would advise you to look at the latest guidance from HMRC and from your accountant, who should be all over this.

In fact, this is a good 'acid test' for your accountant. Ask them about IR35 and see if they do understand it and can explain it to you simply. Remember, it is your responsibility to keep on top of your IR35 status, not your accountant's or your tax adviser's.

You can use the HMRC's helpline to determine your level of exposure to IR35 and if you are successful in getting them to agree you are outside IR35, they will issue you with a certificate and not investigate your for 3 years. However, if you do contact HMRC, you are alerting them to your situation and you go on their records, especially if you are close to be caught by IR35. For this reason, I wouldn't recommend getting in touch with them. Instead, do your own investigation and check yourself against the latest IR35 test.

S660

This is the tax legislation that deals with 'income splitting'. Basically, as you set up your company, you can name your spouse as a fellow Director or Company Secretary and with this, you can decide to split the shares of your company with your spouse. This then allows you to split the dividends payments. In some instances, HMRC argues, these arrangements are done solely for the purposes of minimising the tax for the main earner and maximising the available tax allowance for the spouse – the spouse is not really doing the work, in other words.

Now, there are plenty of contractors doing this but, so far, HMRC has not been able to prosecute. They lost a case (Jones v Garnett – Arctic Systems) in 2007 and have been trying to bring forward legislation since then – so far unsuccessfully, because it is quite difficult for HMRC to argue the case and it is a complex area.

However, the current coalition Government has got this area firmly within their sights, so do beware.

If your spouse does genuinely do Company Secretarial or Director duties, there should be nothing to worry about, as long as you can provide evidence.

BN66

This is legislation that deals with contractors who use offshore tax scheme. If you don't or don't intend to use an offshore vehicle, move on.

If you do, or are intending to, then you're probably well aware of what Government is trying to do. The Finance Act of 2008 states that "UK residents are taxable on their income wherever it arises". So this means that UK residents will pay UK tax on their profits, even it is passes through some foreign partnership arrangement. The tax due is retrospective too – back as far as 1987 – where HMRC can prove the use of the offshore scheme has been a way of avoiding UK taxes.

I have warned you before about off-shore schemes. There are plenty of people out there willing to offer you a scheme that can pay up to 93% of your gross income. Just be aware that the Government is keen on seeing this legislation through.

Agency Workers Regulation (AWR)

This regulation was originally conceived to provide EU member states with a common approach to regulating their temporary labour markets. In some places, temporary labour markets were dominated by vulnerable, low paid and low skilled agency workers, who were frequently abused by hirers or agencies. The regulation came into force in October 2011.

The basis of it is that, after 12 weeks in the same assignment, temporary workers have the same rights as those on permanent contracts of employment in a comparable role. Equal treatment covers pay and working conditions, including overtime, breaks, rest periods and public holidays.

This also includes being made aware of other internal positions that might be coming available.

Contractors are able to benefit from other things too such as minimum wage, paid holidays and the right to work no longer than a 48 hour week.

However, as a contractor, you do not get employee status and therefore cannot claim for unfair dismissal, minimum notice or redundancy pay. These are all usually separately stated in your contract with the agency.

So, you can claim these rights but beware. Under AWR, you are being 'supervised and directed' and not 'controlled', which means that, technically speaking, you can make a claim under AWR and still be outside IR35. However, by claiming these rights, you could be sending a message to HMRC that you are owed rights by the hirer and don't really consider yourself to be a contractor.

It is often the case that contractors who go through agencies are asked to sign away their rights to AWR. This protects the agency, the client and keeps you (potentially) outside IR35.

YOUR FIRST CONTRACT

You've won your contract and you've set up your company and now you're in through the door, what should you be doing?

Plenty. You must continue to make a good impression. Deliver what you said you would deliver and deliver it on time and to good quality. This is the best way to impress but not the only way. In addition, you will have to clearly understand the culture of the working environment you are in. This is different wherever you go. So, all we can do here is give you general guidance notes.

I've structured this into starting your contract, managing the middle of your contract and ending your contract.

Starting your Contract

Roles and Responsibilities

When you start, be clear about your roles and responsibilities. All too often, the agent has interpreted the client's requirements and sometimes can get it round their necks. A good idea is to play the role specification back to the client very early on – Day 1 ideally. This avoids any misinterpretations and gives you a chance to engage the client first hand. The client can also start to give you an idea of where any difficulties might lie.

10 things to ask your client at your first meeting
1.   Who am I reporting to and what is the structure?
2.   What does success look like?
3.   What are my deliverables and in what format?
4.   When are the deliverables needed?
5.   What are the priorities?
6.   What risks are there for me in delivering what you're asking me to deliver?
7.   Who are the key people to talk to (key stakeholders)?
8.   Who is backing this work (who's the sponsor)?
9.   What is my budget?
10.   What resources do I have at my disposal and how good are they?

Once you have the feedback from the client on what you're meant to be doing, write it down and push it back to them for them to check and agree. Then you have a 'contract' with the client.

Managing Holidays

Managing holidays – be clear up front with the client about your holidays. It should have been covered as part of your discussions when negotiating the contract but if not, get this done now. If you are booked into a holiday, there's little a client can do about this other than making you feel bad if it's at an inconvenient time. If you are just taking a breather, you can use this as an "Oh, go on then" type of situation where you agree to change your holidays around to suit your client and thus gain valuable brownie points. A word of warning though. If you've done it once, they may expect you to do it again. It can set a precedent that you don't want to repeat. This is another area that you will want to assess when you first arrive at a client – how do they manage holidays? Don't take too many off so that it causes problems for the client and possibly the permanent staff there – i.e. do they get asked to forgo their holidays when you are free to take them? It's always a tricky balance to achieve and you need to be aware of the client the permanent staff and the needs of the work you are undertaking.

Managing the Client and Key Stakeholders

Now you know what you have to do, you can start to engage with people. It's a good idea to have identified who your key stakeholders are and then meet with them as soon as possible. Be clear as you start to go to these meetings what the purpose is. A good rule of thumb for a meeting is to remember ODA – Objectives, Deliverables and Agenda. Work out ahead of the meeting why you are having the meeting, what you hope to get from it and a list of items for discussion. It's embarrassing if the client comes to one of your meetings and demands to know the objectives and outcomes of the meeting only for you to mumble and be unclear. In my experience, clients remember their first meeting with a new person very well. Try to make it a positive one! Remember, clients' time is valuable – they will not appreciate you wasting their time - at any time.

Assessing the culture is a tricky mix. Generally, keep you eyes and ears open in the first few days and see what goes on. Is it a noisy environment or quiet? Are people pleasant to each other or antagonistic? Is it cooperative or political? Do people start early and leave late? Do people work through lunchtime? Are people fearful of their job security? Is everyone busy or is it patchy? Do people communicate well with each other? Is there a team ethos around the place?

By answering these types of questions, you can quickly get a view on what is going on in a company or department and tailor your approach accordingly. This is a key part of the skill set of a contractor – how quickly you can work out a client way of working and how best to fit in. If you do make any errors in the early part of your contract – apologise to the client. This is crucial. It shows you're aware and that you appreciate you did something wrong and that you are sorry and it won't happen again.

No-one expects you to be the life and soul of the party but it absolutely helps if you get on with people. Even if you have to grin and bear it! Trust me, it happens a lot. Keep everyone sweet and you can look forward to a long and profitable contract.

Be wary of jumping to conclusions or being overly critical of the client's current situation or past performance. You don't know until you are well embedded who you might be offending. I find it very useful to feed back my initial impressions to the client at the end of the first week. This way, the client has an opportunity to put you straight and give you some background – and often some tutoring/lecturing! It's all an important part of fitting in, delivering and managing all the right people.

Managing the middle of your Contract

Asking for a rate rise

So everything is going along swimmingly. You've been in the job for a while and you're fitting in well with the culture, the boss is happy with your delivery and is valuing your contribution. You're feeling bold and are thinking about asking for a rate rise. This could be because you went in at a rate that you know undervalues what you're doing and this was all part of the plan or because they've started to ask you to take on more responsibility or because you're coming to a new phase in the work or because you're coming to the end of your current contract and you know they are going to want to extend you into a new contract. Where do you start?

Depends. If you are going through a consultancy firm that takes an active interest in your day to day well being, you will need to talk with them first so that they can either go to the client and ask for a rate rise or they can decide to take less margin on your rate and just give you the rate rise without bothering the client. If you are going through an agent, who basically does nothing more than pay you each month and you never see them (happens in most cases!), then you can approach the client directly and make your case to them. If they agree, then you can contact the agent and tell them the good news, which is you've just got a rise and they should be grateful because you've just increased their fee (usually based on a percentage of your pay, remember!).

Don't be greedy. At the lower end, if you're on an hourly rate of say £15/hr, then to go to £18-20/hr is a big percentage rate rise but amounts to £300-500/month, which may be a no-brainer for a client if they really want to keep you. For a mid-range day rate, say £400/day, trying to ask for more than a £50/day rate rise might be pushing it. But if you've been brought on as a project manager and you've been asked to take on the programme manager role then you would be quite within your rights to ask for the rate at or near what other programme managers are typically getting paid.

If you're on an hourly rate, quite often the client will want to move everyone on to a day rate. This reduces variability in the salary bill and allows for more accurate planning. This is a good opportunity to secure a rise. It depends again on how much variability there is on your working day. So if you consistently do 8 hours per day, then the client is easily going to convert that via a simple multiple and come up with a day rate figure. If you work between 8-10 hours every day, then you should aim to get your day rate based on the 10 hours per day or a middle position after negotiation. Either way, you end up knowing what you're going to get paid and you're going to get paid at least as much as your contract says.

Coping with Change during a Contract

Change happens, get used to it. One thing to work out early on in a new client is how they deal with their contractors. Are they afforded respect and is there an inclusive approach to having contractors on site or not? So, do contractors get invited to team events, evenings out, company debriefs, that sort of thing. There are in my mind very many advantages to a more inclusive approach. It means that everyone is working on the same set of information, especially if there is big change or restructuring going off in a company, which, let's face it, happens just about everywhere these days. Even so, some clients do treat contractors a little bit like second class citizens. Contractors are a necessary evil, only there because they have a temporary requirement driven by the amount of change in their company. Ideally, contractors wouldn't be there, they're expensive and the sooner they can get rid of them the better. So, flog them and don't give them even an hour "slack" to slope off into some company debrief! So observing this is crucial because you may get in the line of fire and you need to be prepared for it.

In the worst cases, clients can just decide that they've had enough of having contractors around and they issue notice there and then. Most often, you get your contractually obliged termination period (most often 4 weeks), but in some extreme cases, you can be asked to leave in a few days. If you see this happening to other contractors, be prepared. Recently, there has been the rise in popularity of 'zero-notice' contracts. As it says on the tin, there is no notice period either way. So you can decide you've had enough on a Friday and not turn up for work on the Monday. Equally, the client can have the same change of heart. In my opinion, this drives entirely the wrong kind of behaviour but we warned, there are more and more zero notice contracts appearing.

Change happens for all sorts of reasons. The biggest driver of a change in my experience is a new boss coming in higher up the chain. If you're sponsor changes, get ready for a different approach. Watch how your immediate boss reacts. Are they edgy, how are they engaging with the new arrival? Are they going to be in favour with the new regime? Are they distancing themselves? Worst case, they're phoning up agents and asking you about contracting opportunities!!

If your immediate boss changes, get ready for change. Their frame of reference can be different from that of your existing boss and they will want to make an impact when they arrive. So understand why your boss is moving on, seek reassurance from them as to who the new person is and what they are likely to do or have been asked to do. You can then make your mind up as to your course of action – if you see a risk to you, then you should be starting to look for other opportunities (see later).

Managing Teams during a Contract

This is a tricky one and the approach is determined by your personality, the client, the teams you are managing and the culture in the company. I've managed teams comprised of permanent staff, teams comprised wholly of contract staff and combinations of the two. Primarily, I think this is driven by you. My personal belief is that if I am managing permanent staff, then I should take on the role of their manager and be their mentor, trainer and promoter in the business. So, I believe I should know about their promotion procedures and their prospects. However, the client should have procedures in place to deal with this type of situation so it is important that you check with them in the first place.

For permanent staff, if the client has other people who will act as your staff's counsellor/mentor, then your job is to know what their mentor is asking your staff to achieve – to understand their personal development plans and what targets they are being asked to achieve for the year in order for them to be successful. Once you have discussed this with their mentor, you should agree how you will go about achieving it and agree that with your team member. That way, you are aligned and trying your best to make sure they are going to be successful by working with you. It also enables you to manage in training and development needs and ensures these are not a surprise.

If the client has no real mentoring system in place, then it does come back on you and what you believe you can do to help your team be successful. A key question I ask is "What are you trying to get out of this piece of work/assignment/job?" or "What does being successful look like to you in this piece of work/assignment/job?" Sometimes, people have never been asked this question before and they may struggle with an answer. So don't be surprised if it takes a while to get a well formed response! I've had all sorts come back to me from these questions. "I want to work in the UN" from an analyst "I'm just here to learn as much as I can before I go and set up another company" from a junior team member, "I want to learn how to run projects so I can be in charge and be a programme manager" from an administrator, "I just want to learn how to do what I do better and I think you can help me" from lots of people!

Once you have a good reply from your team member, you can work out how best to help them. Whatever gap you are trying to fill, get them to identify the steps they need to take to achieve them and then put dates and action owners (most of which should be them) against each step. This way, they can work out themselves if they are being realistic or not.

I say to many people "It's no longer a case of what you can do for your company, more a case of what the company can do for you". If you come at your work with this kind of mentality, then it's surprising how you change your approach. As I have mentioned before, there aren't many advantages for being employed, in my opinion, but one clear advantage is the training and development opportunities they can enjoy. So get them to enjoy them – get your team on as many training courses as you can. You will be helping them out a great deal and giving them the best potential opportunity for their future development.

For contract staff, the approach is similar but potentially less formal. I ask my contract team what they want to get out of the engagement. What is it that I can help them with? If they can't answer, that's not great but not necessarily a surprise. It's quite rare that contractors get asked, "Why are you here?" The answer generally is because they got the job to pay the bills to keep going – quite a lot of contractors don't really have too many aims and objectives other than to get more experience under their belt so they can get a better rate and to keep in employment or avoid times of unemployment. If their answer is based on rate and employability, then there's not a lot you can do. But very now and then, my contractors are clear that they want to work in one of my teams to see how it is done well and properly and that they can take this experience elsewhere and use it again. Occasionally, my contractors will ask that I specifically help them in a certain area – clarity of writing reports, stakeholder management, or in a specific process that they have never done before. Again, with each of these areas, I get them to write down the steps they need to take to achieve their aims and add in timescales and action owners. We then agree the plan and we stick to it.

Coping with a rate reduction

In the world of equities, the phrase "your investment value can go up as well as down" can be equally applied to your rate in contracting. Be prepared is the best advice I can give you. Rate reductions are thankfully not that common but they can be implemented with alarming speed by certain clients. I have known clients that have put a blanket 10% reduction on contractor rates almost overnight. There is very little you can do about this. You may think that because you have a contract in place that affords you some protection. It doesn't. You can try and fight it, but you will lose and generally it will not be worth your while. It would be very unusual to hear of a rate reduction of more than 10%. You have two options – stay or go. Stay and you put up and shut up. You will be asked to sign up to a new contract and a lot of contractors will just shrug their shoulders and take the hit. They know that if they try to move and they don't find a job quickly, then any reduction in rate is quickly wiped out by not earning for a few days. Quick example, a contractor on £400/day is asked to take a 10% reduction – so loses £40/day. Over a 3 month period (typical contract extension), this amounts to £2,400 (60 working days). So if they leave a job and take more than 6 days to get into a new contract, then they will be losing out. So it depends on how quickly you are being told that you are moving to the new rate as to how you handle it. I have never been in this situation but I would say two things. You should at all times be aware of the climate in which you are operating. You should be sufficiently well connected and should be able to see this kind of thing coming. Second, if you do get caught by surprise, and a rate reduction is on the cards, then try to negotiate an exception from your client and if they refuse, leave. You are not a charity case. If they reduce rates and won't negotiate on your behalf, then I don't believe they should have the benefit of you being around. And if this drops them in trouble, tough. Their decision. But I will always advise, leave graciously. Do not open your mouth and start shouting the odds and being provocative. How you act in these situations is of paramount importance. Your reputation is key. Do not put this at risk when leaving. I just think of moving on as being exciting – a step into the unknown, something new to do, new relationships to forge... great!

Managing the end of your Contract

This brings us nicely on to how to manage things when you are getting close to the end of a contract. This is an area where a lot of new contractors fear to tread. It's where I get most calls and questions and concerns.

Understanding Seasonality in the Contractor Marketplace

Before we get into the options that face you when moving on from a contract, it is important to consider the timing of your move and for this, you need to understand the seasonality of the contractor marketplace.

In contracting there is definitely a good time and a bad time to be changing roles.

January/February - in January the market is dead in the first 2 weeks. If a client is going to place a role for the New Year, they will have generally done it before Christmas, if they're organised. So in the first couple of weeks of the New Year, we're dealing with those who didn't get round to it or who got round to it but couldn't find anyone. A lot of contracts do run to a year end and there can be a lot of people looking for roles in the New Year. They had Christmas off, they've had a nice time, spent way to much, earned no fees and are now rabidly looking for work. But the agents need their break and they're not back and in gear again until the end of the first week. Then they need to get the paperwork sorted with the client and place the advertisement. We're into the second or third week in January before things pick up.

March – the market picks up steadily until March, when all hell breaks loose and people are hiring like crazy. There's a lag in the system usually driven by clients getting their new annual budgets approved. Once they get the go ahead, they run around getting business cases sorted and resource plans signed off and it's March before they hit the market. Then BOOM! Off we go. It's brief – Easter kills the market stone dead. Then there's another hiatus as we move towards the summer.

April/May/June - Late April, May and early June are good times for contractors. Companies are hiring ahead of the summer and ensuring they have enough people on board before…

July/August - …we move into what many call the 'silly season'. This is when schools break up and the 'decision-making' clients are going on holiday. It all grinds to a halt again! The end of July, August and into the early part of September is a contractor hiring 'dead-zone'. August is particularly bad.

September to November - Then we're off again. Everyone comes back after the summer and get their teeth back into delivery. They start hiring again and off we go. This lasts until mid to late November, when the market winds down again.

December - There are opportunities in December but come mid-December, we're back in the dead-zone again.

So the key thing here is to recognise that there is not a constant supply or demand of contractors during the year. To maximise your chance of keeping a regular income, you need to think ahead to the 'dead-zones' in the year. Danger signals are with those contracts that end in July, August or at the end of the year – November or December. In these situations, you really need to think ahead. You need to ask more questions of the client early – is there likely to be an extension? If so, for how long? Are there other opportunities internally? Either on the project of elsewhere? If the answer to these is "No", then you must crank up your contacts early and start to let people know you are coming available for work.

Minimising the Risk to moving between Contracts

The right thing to do is to plan for a bit of down time between contracts. This certainly eases the pressure on you to secure a new role. Only you can work out what this means for you. Let's suppose you might end up with – worst case – 4 weeks between contracts. You've come off a 6 month contract. You should keep between 15% - 20% aside to cater for this. Surprisingly high number and tricky not to touch it as you go through.

Suppose you're on £400/day. Over 6 months, you will invoice around £43,000 (assuming 18 days/month – taking holidays into account). Taking a month out to secure another job means you need around £7,000 to keep you going (pro-rata). This works out to 16.6% so between 15% and 20% is a safe bet depending on your attitude to risk and general nervous disposition. I always advise people to do this and yet I don't do this myself! I wing it horribly and have very little in reserve, so the pressure on me is ridiculous when it comes to changing contracts, but it's still a bit of a hoot – I liken it to Tarzan swinging through the jungle on a vine – each vine is a contract. As you get on to a new vine, it's a hairy ride, you accelerate quickly not really knowing where you're heading or what obstacles lie in your path, then things calm down as you reach the bottom of your swing and everything's in order and the speed is constant, with the maximum amount of pressure on you. Then finally, on the upswing, you're thinking about moving on, the contract's coming to an end and you're looking out for the next vine to leap on to. It's all about timing! Sometimes the vine is there and you grab it, leaving the old one behind just as you accelerate like billy-o on the new vine. Sometimes it ain't there and you end up on the jungle floor for a while, until you painstakingly climb a big old tree and get yourself onto the next vine. Sometimes, it takes such a long time getting back up the tree, you opt for a lower vine and it swings much more quickly (lower rate and shorter term contract!), but it gets you back in the race and keeps you off the jungle floor!

One more thing, don't get into thinking, "Oh, it's all ok because I work a month ahead and I've still got an invoice to be paid for the last month that I worked" – that unravels the next month, when you have to work your first month, then invoice and, ah, don't get paid for 30 days! Do be careful with this, especially if you are moving form being paid weekly to being paid monthly. It's great getting the money in more regularly, but you only have one week at the end of the contract when you will get paid, so all the more reason to put some reserves aside.

The next contract – remember, it's more difficult to keep tracks on securing your new contract when you are already in a contract. As soon as you are requested to get paperwork to your new agents/clients DO IT! Keep on it, keep checking progress. All too often, things slip and you might be able to negotiate staying on a little while at your exiting client while things sort themselves out at the new client.

References – Another good reason to leave on good terms is that you are more likely to get a decent reference, although, these days, employers are more limited when it comes to providing detailed references as I mentioned earlier.

Managing the client as you move on – Do let key people know that you are moving on. Sometimes, it's worth informing a few really key people unofficially before you let everyone know. Do send out an email to all the people that you've been working with, wishing them well and offering for them to stay in touch and provide your contact details. Sometimes it can be a good idea to do two lists – the second one, a much more focused list in which you do include your future contact details and the first one, where you don't! Your call.

Do arrange a few drinks. It's interesting to find out who can be bothered to make the effort to come out to say thank you and goodbye and who can't. This equally applies to inviting people out for a meal. Judge what you do in this regard by how long you've been there and where you sit in the hierarchy. If you set the whole thing up and have been there for a while, it's quite common for the client to formally say thank you by arranging a full blown leaving do for you. Don't expect it, but it's nice when it happens. I've been fortunate enough to have had a number of really very nice evenings out at the end of contracts, with prizes and presents!

It's worth remembering to treat others as you would like to be treated yourself. If one of your team is leaving, do make an appropriate fuss (which may be nothing of course!). Do be careful if someone is leaving under a cloud. If the exit is justified, my advice is leave it to them to decide what they want to do. Just think about "what comes around, goes around".

Options for Changing your Contract

There aren't too many options when it comes to the end of your contract but what is absolutely critical is simply to plan ahead. Planning ahead can save you thousands of pounds in lost revenue. You want to give yourself ample time to work out what you want to do. Simply, this is:

1. stay as you are,
2. do something different or take on a new role at the same client or
3. move to a new opportunity.

Whichever route you choose, the timing is driven by how long it can take you to get into a new role. Think about the steps for getting into a new role and work back. It takes

-   a week to get contracts in place
-   a week for a client to make up their mind
-   a week to arrange an interview and get you through an interview
-   a good 2-3 weeks for your network to know you're on the market and find an opportunity that might suit you

So, simply put, if you don't want a gap between contracts (some people do use time in between contracts as an opportunity for a breather), then 5-6 weeks prior to the end of your contract, put the word out. You are coming available.

So, it's important that you start discussions with the client about 6-8 weeks ahead of your planned end of contract, in order that you can make a reasoned choice.

Stay where you are

In this case, you need to engage the client in a discussion about your continued role in the team. Your contract is a few weeks away from ending and you need to know from the client what their intentions are. Is the work going to continue? Do they still need your role? Do they still see the need for you in your role or are they keen to find someone new? If all this is positive, then the questions you need to ask are about responsibilities, duration of new contract and rate.

Yes rate! At every point of change, there is the possibility to negotiate a new improved rate to continue your contract. Only you can judge the situation. You may think you're onto a good thing and that rocking the boat is not a good idea. But if you do want to have a go, there are various ways of going about it.

Your argument can be:
- You're pretty indispensible or added significant value
- They would find it hard to get a replacement for you in the time
- They know you and you know how they work
- You aren't currently getting paid as much as some of your peers
- You only need a token increase (assuming this is true)
- You've been working over and above your job description

But do judge the situation. It's always useful to get to know the other contractors on your project and other projects and see if they will let you know if they managed to secure an increase. If they all got a flat 'NO', then you should not see this as a reason not to ask, because if you don't ask, you definitely will not get, more a way of managing your own expectation. Of course, if they did all get a 'NO', then you might see this as a reason to look around in any case.

If your responsibilities, duration of new contract and rate are all acceptable to you, then agree timescales with the client to get a new contract in place and inform your agent.

Same Client, Different Role

This is pretty much the same as the approach for staying as you are (above) but in this case, you need to agree the exact nature of your new role, documented preferably, your rate and the contract duration. Again, if you are taking on more responsibility, then do take the opportunity to explore a rate increase with your client. It's worthwhile knowing the other contractors that are in similar roles to work out where to pitch your new rate but make sure you're going to get a rate that you're comfortable with given the role. There is nothing worse than flogging your guts out day after day, evening after evening, thinking you're not getting a decent recompense for what you're doing.

Again, once your responsibilities, duration of the contract and rate are all acceptable to you, agree timescales to get the new contract in place and inform your agent.

Move to a New opportunity

In this instance, I would still advise having the conversation with the client about future potential contract extensions about 6-8 weeks before your contract is due for renewal. Even if they want you to stay, you may have had enough and want to move on yourself, but it's nice to know there is a backup in case you don't find anything. If they want you to move on, it's a no brainer – you're moving.

Moving on from a client is to be carefully managed. How you exit reflects on you and your brand and reputation. So it's important you get it right. First, you need to have made up your mind that you are indeed going to move on. But you don't need to tell anyone else at this stage. Your contract will typically require you to give 4 weeks notice to the client. So, by engaging the client at 6-8 weeks out, you're giving yourself a bit of breathing space (2-4 weeks) to find out what is out there in the market.

Alternatively, let's assume you've had the chat with the client and they don't want you to stay beyond the contract. You're 6-8 weeks away from not being paid a cent. That generally focuses people's minds! But no need to panic. Here's what you need to do.

a. You need to figure out if you are still marketing yourself under the same job role – so if you have always branded yourself as a project manager, do you now have enough experience to call yourself a programme manager? This is important because it fixes specific roles in the mind of the agent and others whom you're about to contact

b. You need to determine what rate you are looking for. Is it higher than last time you looked? If so, why? Will the market stand the rate you're after?

c. You need to determine in which location you are prepared to look for a new contract. Is this the same as previously or can you go country-wide or international.

d. You need to be clear about your start date. Is it the Monday after you finish the previous job or are you going to have a few days/weeks off?

    Once you've answered these questions, you can start to look for roles. In my case, when changing roles, I'm usually sticking to the same role, trying to get a better rate, but being flexible on location and on timing. This gives your agency contacts bit of freedom when it comes to narrowing down the potential options for you.

Update your CV. This needs to have your current role on it to bring it bang up to date. Make any other alterations you need to do. One of my protégés often tinkers with his CV just to keep it fresh. It's a good idea to keep reviewing it and keep it up to date.

The next step is to fire up your network – we're still 6-8 weeks away from changing but it's important to start early. The people you know, the agents you know and the people you have worked with on your current contract are all potential sources for your next job. And don't forget that your existing client is probably one of the best potential providers of your next role. You worked there, you're familiar with the culture, you know who's who and how to get things done there, so just because your current boss doesn't want you, it shouldn't stop you from trying to find another boss in the same company.

Then you're into the same old situation. Chasing leads, moving things forward, getting on top of people, relentlessly following up new opportunities – all this while you're working! Do be careful. Don't make it so obvious that you're on your way out by taking calls at your desk. Be as private and as discreet as you can be. You do not want to hack you existing boss off just as you walk out of the door. After all, you may need them to give you a reference. So take calls at lunch time, early in the morning, early in the evening. Do check your emails, but do it carefully. Do not use the client email to look for your new job. Keep all correspondence going to your private email address. After all, you're still being paid to work not job search.

I enjoy the chase! The thrill of not really knowing where you're going to end up next. It's all down to timing and in the lap of the Gods – a great deal is down to fate! I use this time to refresh my contacts and make new ones. It's a great opportunity to expand your network. Meet new agents, additional sources of new work. You just have to love it! Remember Tarzan, I'm often hanging on to the bitter end, no vine in sight that's going to be strong enough to support me – but somehow, acrobatically, I manage to steer myself into a part of the jungle, mid-flight, where there are decent vines and BINGO, leap like a gazelle just in time! All about your attitude to risk! If you're disciplined financially, you can manage contract changes easily.

And that's the trick. Keeping off the jungle floor. But only you can weigh up the options that will come your way. Many times, I've been in the situation of "a bird in the hand is worth two in the bush". If you have an opportunity that is ok but not quite perfect, you have to work out if it's worth taking it anyway. There's some simple maths again – suppose you're on £400/day and you're sticking out for an extra £50/day and you can have a role at your existing rate now or get a contract for the increased rate after 3 weeks. Financially, it makes sense to take the job at the lower rate now. In the intervening 3 weeks that you wait for the increased rate, you could have earned £6000. At the increased rate, it will take you 120 days to break even! Or 6 months! Ouch – don't do it – keep the continuity going, even if it does bruise your ego!

Weighing up the options doesn't just extend to the rate though. It's about your work life balance, proximity to home, ease of getting to the client site, the nature of the work you'd be doing. All of these have to be balanced against each other for you to reach the best conclusion for you. And remember, you're a contractor, so if you don't like where you ended up, just move on again – just don't do it too often! I do lists of pros and cons, I talk to my family and trusted friends who know me well and tell me if I'm going down the wrong path. It is good to talk.

So back to your existing client. Once you do have a new role in place, then you should tell them as soon as you can. If you can, make sure the new contracts are in place before you tell your existing client. However, more often than not, you don't get this luxury, so you will almost certainly be giving them notice without everything being completely sorted. Therefore there is risk.

It can be a difficult conversation with your client, so make sure you work out the best timing – take them off somewhere private and be prepared for several potential outcomes.

Some clients when faced with your imminent departure may try to keep hold of you. They may try increasing your rate, contract duration, even role to try to keep you. Be warned though. If you have been through a selection process with another client and they have selected you and you have verbally said "yes", even if the contracts aren't signed, sealed and delivered, I would strongly advise against changing your mind. If you do, it looks like you played one client off against another and you can and will get a reputation for that. Agents will be wary to represent you in future – it really isn't worth it. At this point it is best to remember:

Your word is your bond

Some clients can get quite distressed at your departure, especially if they have relied upon you heavily. So be aware that they may become angry at the situation. You just need to stick to the facts and tell them as sympathetically as you can that you are moving on and when that is going to happen.

If you end up not having a clear opportunity to go to but you are convinced you are going to leave, things can get quite tricky. You can be faced with not having given notice and coming up to a month away from the end of your contract. It is your call if you want the contract to run out and do nothing about it. The client has a responsibility to make sure they are on top of their contract staff. If you are going to leave, then you still need to be clear with your client about your intentions. After all, it's you that has decided to move on and if the client has to get someone else in to replace you, they are going to need around 4 weeks to get the right person. Strictly speaking, as you get towards a month away from the end of your contract, the client should be coming to you asking what you intend to do in order for them to maintain their team. But don't rely on this. A lot of clients don't really keep a detailed eye on when their contractor end dates are, so be proactive. Remember, it's your reputation at stake as you exit any contract, and you must do this professionally.

If, for whatever reason, you don't give notice and don't sign a new contract, then you can turn up on the client's site and work but you will be doing so at risk until you get the contract signed. Some clients won't even let you on site until the contract is signed for legal and liability reasons.

Delivering a Professional Exit

Whatever happens, you **have** to deliver a professional exit. You cannot bad mouth the place or the people and you should continue to work hard and deliver what you promise. I've said it so often "what goes around, comes around". Keep your mouth shut when moving on. If you don't, you run the risk of meeting up with that person in the future or risk offending a friend or an ally of them. Remember, your reputation is absolutely key to you. It's your brand, you have to protect it at all costs. It's what sets you apart from loads of other contractors.

10 points for a professional exit
1. Still delivering on time
2. Still going the extra mile, staying focused on the outcomes, not the clock
3. Not taking relentless phone calls from agents offering you new opportunities
4. Not getting frustrated or venting your frustration – just because you're going
5. Continuing to look after your team or continuing to be part of your team
6. Continuing to make professional decisions
7. Doing a great handover (see separate handover list criteria)
8. Letting your key stakeholders know, professionally, that you are moving on
9. Not taking long lunch breaks suddenly
10. Not distracting people or lauding it over people who are staying

BUILDING YOUR BUSINESS AND MAXIMISING YOUR INCOME

It is up to how you run and build your business. That's the beauty of it. You decide how much effort you are going to put into it, how much marketing you do, what the standards are, what your standards are, which industries you target, what you spend your money on etc.

There are lots of things that are important and I'm not going to dictate to you how you decide to build your business but here are a few helpful things to think about.

Setting and Maintaining Standards

Every day you leave the house or your hotel, you are your brand. Everything you do is going to have a positive or a negative impact on that. Your standards are up to you now. If you arrive late, what does that say about you. If you are scruffy or your shoes are dirty, what image does that conjure up in the mind of the client? If you are disorganised, if you're too loud, if you swear too much, if you lose your temper, whatever it may be, it all reflects on you now and your brand. As a permanent member of staff, you can get away with quite a lot before an employer would think about dismissing you. As a contractor, well, one foot wrong and they can just say, "Sorry, 1 month's notice. See you!"

Do bear in mind some obvious things in the table below – they're all common sense aren't they? The only trouble with common sense though, it isn't too common! Stick to these simple truths and you will do better than 90% of people, perm or contractor.

10 Standards to adopt as a contractor
1. Reply to emails
2. Work hard and deliver on time
3. Don't swear at work (not in front of the client anyway!)
4. Be good fun, get on with people, be serious if you need to be and keep your promises
5. Turn up on time
6. Dress smartly
7. Be tidy and organised
8. Stick to the first arrangement (don't ditch for another better offer!)
9. Don't bitch about people
10. Keep in touch with people

Keeping and expanding your network

Your network is about the most powerful thing you need to develop as you go contracting. It's like an allotment. For it to flourish and produce good yields, it needs to be constantly tended. You must apply a liberal amount of fertiliser (money, drinks, food!) to cultivate it – in the nicest possible way!

You have to make the effort. Now you're out on your own, your brand and your reputation are the most important thing you possess above others in the same field. To some extent this is conferred by the people who you work with, who you want to work with and who you associate with. The objective is not to have the largest network in the world, the objective is to build a trusted group of people around you, people you know you could work with and who would work with you again and again.

It's definitely worth being careful who you let into your network. Using a business network site like LinkedIn for example. This is becoming the network to belong to and it's also turning into a large recruitment site. Agents go there and scour it day after day, narrowing down people against their specific requirements. But remember, when you let people into your network, they can see all your contacts, so be careful who you let in. Don't confuse your business network with your social network. They may be very close and in some instances overlap – some of your best work buddies can become real good friends. So why wouldn't they be on your LinkedIn and Facebook sites?

People say I'm really good at keeping in touch. The truth is my phone has 885 contacts (I just checked!) but the number of people I would trust to work with again is less than 100. I keep the names of people on my phone pretty much forever. I encourage you to put as much detail as you can on your phone about them depending on how you remember them. I'm great at remembering faces and lousy about putting names to faces, so having a photo or at least a client name where you worked together is a must. After 9 or 10 years, even the sharpest memory can fade, so give yourself a chance!

Your network should grow each time you move on – one of the benefits of moving around! How's this work then? Well, you move on, you talk to the people that got you your first jobs. They might not instantly be able to find an opportunity so it forces you to ask other people – outside of your network. But once you have made contact, they know about you, they become part of your network. But you must work to retain them in your network. I don't claim that my network is 885 strong (contacts on my phone) my network is about 100 people – the people I can phone, text, email who would actively look for another job for me or who might know someone else who might be able to help. And that has taken a number of years to develop. It has been cultivated and I know when I'm not cultivating it enough.

You know the people in your trusted network - you talk to them or see them at least once a quarter. Sounds too little? OK, work it out across 100 people, that's 400 interactions a year – or **one new conversation A DAY** with someone you haven't spoken to for 3 months. Now I know I don't do that, so I know I'm not tending my network as I should. Makes you think! Look at your recent calls on your phone. Take away family and immediate friends, how many people in your network have you called in the last month. Bet it's not 30!

Point is it's good to talk. It's amazing what comes about just because you're keeping in touch with people. It shows you care and it shows you don't just call them up when you need a job – treat them as you would your friends, after all, a lot of them will be!

It's important to keep your LinkedIn or business network up to date with what you're doing too. Every new role is an opportunity to let people know how you're doing. LinkedIn sends a message out every time you update your latest position. So it's an invite to people to get in touch. If you don't update, they don't know you moved. If you don't move that regularly, find a reason to get your name out and about – favourite ways of doing this are updating your skills, connecting to other people or sending a link to a new article.

In marketing, they would call it maintaining 'Top of Mind Awareness' or TOMA. You should aim to regularly pop up in front of your network.

Maximising your Earning Potential

The amount to which you can maximise your earnings is directly related to how much spare time you have available or can generate. Doing client work can take up a huge amount of time, especially as you become more senior – it is expected that you will go above and beyond to deliver what you need to do. This leaves you with little time, generally, to do other things. But it's not impossible. It's about carving out time and being disciplined with it.

There are a number of things you can do to earn extra income or increase your day rate.

Contract Change – this is the most obvious way of getting your rate up. Each and every time you change your contract, even if it's just extending your contract, you should be thinking about increasing your rate. I say thinking about it, because it's not always the case that it's appropriate to be asking for a rate rise. You have to be aware of and sensitive to the situation you're in. If perms are being made redundant, if more experienced contractors are not achieving rate increases, if contractors are being let go and not being replaced, then these are all signs that the client is going to be unlikely to respond well to a request for an increased rate.

However, you must give it thought and even the smallest rate rise counts. An extra £25/day is another £500/month, which helps! And when it comes to moving on, you will always be asked your current rate. If you can say you were extended and achieved a rate rise on a project, then it looks really good to an agent and allows you to position yourself at a potentially higher rate as a starting point.

Responsibility Change – another reason to ask about rate increase. If you are taking on more responsibility or the client is asking you to do something different from what you were originally contracted to do, then rate absolutely comes into question. Again, take into account other contractors in similar roles. If you're at the top end of the rate band for that role, then you might be pushing it but if you're at the lower end, make a case by comparing yourself and your skills and experience to others in similar roles.

Writing Papers and Speaking at Conferences – these are both good ways to expanding your network, heightening your personal brand and thus increasing your 'net worth' and potentially your rate. Clearly, you need to be in a position of some authority to be able to deliver on either of these but it looks great on your CV and clients will be impressed. If you do too much of this, the only thing to watch out for is that clients may label you as 'academic' and may see this as something that could cause interruption to your availability. So, if you can venture into this space, make sure you achieve an appropriate balance with delivery.

Delivering Training – it may be possible to turn what you have delivered with a client into a training course and deliver this to an invited, fee paying, audience. Again, you need to be careful to balance the time you spend delivering training versus time on client site. If you deliver training courses at the weekend, this should not create a problem. Do be careful about intellectual property (IP) ownership. Typically, whilst on a client site, any IP generated belongs to the client. Sometimes, the IP belongs to the agent or consultancy firm you contract through. Occasionally, if this is not covered, it belongs to you but do be careful not to infringe the client's rights. However, you can either be open with your client and let then know what you're going to do or you can write the training course generically, without making reference to the client specifically and if this works, there should be no IP issues.

Bringing new people into a contract - so you're in a contract and you think you can see an opportunity to bring someone in that you know and trust. Maybe there's a gap in the team, or someone's leaving or a new role opens up. You think, I know just the person to cover that. The simplest way of getting that person in, is to mention it to your line manager and see what their reaction is. If they are positive, then you may want to make the introduction, put your boss and your friend together and let things run their course. That's the simple way, you're just being helpful.

The tricky part comes when money gets involved. You think, I can bring my friend in and I can make some money out of this. Good for you for being entrepreneurial but there are some things you should do if you go down this route. The simple route is that you make the introduction, but you do it via an agency. It pre-supposes that you have built a pretty good relationship with your and other agencies. The role needs to be confirmed and placed with the client's agents. You should mention to your boss that you have someone in mind for the role and that you are going to recommend they apply for the role through the agent. Then you contact the agency and introduce your friend to them on condition that you will earn a "finder's fee". This can range from zero, some agencies just don't do this, to a meal out or up to a few hundred pounds depending on the rate and duration of the contract position. You can obviously do an internal selling job on your boss as your friend goes through the selection process and this can sometimes help significantly.

The more complex route is when you try to get a slice of the day rate to come your way via your own company. So, your mate is coming to work for the client through your company. This presupposes that the client does not have a Preferred Supplier List in place and that they are happy to take your recommendation. In practise, with larger companies, this is rarely the case these days. The best advice is to be absolutely clear and transparent with your client. Tell them that you have someone, let them know that you are happy for them to come through your company and even talk to them about margins that you would apply and let them make the decision. If they're ok with it, then you can go ahead.

Remember you are taking some risk here. By using a sub-contractor, you will need to get a contract in place with them, you will need to understand and protect yourself from any potential claims from the client, in case your buddy doesn't work out, and you have to pay your buddy, even if the client hasn't paid you. So pay close attention to their payment terms. It can be a lot of hassle for little reward, but eventually, if you can get a few people on board like this, it can mount up and suddenly, you're an agency!

Becoming an Associate of a Consulting Firm - this is almost the holy grail. This is where you just happen to have a skill set that a consultancy firm doesn't have or doesn't have enough of. Firms can invite you to be an 'associate', which means you still remain an independent contractor but you work through them. They often brand you as one of their own, you often get their business cards, you get invited along to nights out, you get to build a network within their company. But you don't get their company perks, their training or their company away days. It's effectively a layer between you and the client, similar to them acting as an agent on your behalf. They will charge you out at 'consultancy rates' and pay you your contractor day rate. So, they will do well out of you because they don't have to pay all the overhead of a permanent employee.

The beauty of it is that, if they have good relationships with several clients, and you do well for them, then they can see you as a flexible resource that can be positioned in many places and they don't have to worry too much about if it's the right level or if it's going to get you promoted. They just pay you your day rate and you get on with it! And they often get to do great pieces of work that the client can't put with the big boys because they're just too expensive or it's politically not the right thing to be doing at that time.

Don't go thinking this is an easy win or an early win. You will have to build up a reputation in your area of specialism and then know the right people who can introduce you as an associate. The good firms don't rely too much on associates – they will have a handful only.

I've worked for a smaller consultancy firm in such an arrangement and it works well. You need to keep in touch with the people that brought you into the firm because you might not end up working directly with them. This is especially true when coming up to the end of your contract. It's the same process as described earlier when working with an agent. You need to find out if the contract is likely to be extended and for how long and where you are likely to be working next. I ensure that I get a feel for the nature of the culture of the firm too. Then, you just try to fit in. If you are not difficult to manage and get on and deliver, then they are more likely to keep you on. How much you get involved with the firm is up to you. The more involved you get, the more you are likely to become a 'fixture' and perhaps inevitably, you may get offered a job with them. If that works for you, then great. Just use this checklist to ensure they're worth sticking with:

10 Characteristics of Good Smaller Consulting Firms
1. They have a good but steady growth strategy
2. They care about their consultants
3. They have regular in-house and external training courses
4. They have an annual appraisal and performance development system in place and it works
5. They have very well connected senior management with a good range of top quality clients
6. Their fees are not exorbitant
7. Their salaries are fair and there is a good bonus system in place
8. They have a good internal social network
9. They expect their consultants to own and develop areas of competency within the firm
10. They don't expect their consultants to constantly work excessively long hours or regularly work weekends

Some consultancy firms work like this and others don't – just ferret out the ones that do and strike up a relationship with them. It takes a lot of effort, commitment and investment to satisfy the criteria above. It most definitely is not for the faint hearted.

A word of caution – there are some companies out there that want to make the transition from being agents to being full blown consultancy firms. The margins move from about 15%-20% to about 40%. That's the incentive for them – they will make a shed load more cash if they get it right. However, in my experience, the companies who are able to do this are few and far between. You need a different breed of people in a consultancy to those in an agency associate network. The acid test comes down to the background of the people running the agency, their contacts and their client bank. If they've been in a consultancy environment for a good few years and have always plotted a route into their own consultancy firm via an agency, there's a chance it will come off. An agency thinking they can just move into this space will inevitably struggle. Be warned, and be wary of promises made to you. It is up to you to make the judgement.

LOOKING AFTER YOURSELF

It's important to keep looking after yourself. You may do this quite well already. A large number of contractors that I know pride themselves in the number of days that they **haven't** taken off through illness over the years. There's a lot of pride in this figure. Ask a dyed in the wool contractor how many days they've had off ill over the last year and they will know it instantly. And the answer is invariably zero, one or two days. When you go to work as a contractor, there's a kind of unwritten rule that you will be at work come what may. And this is great for revenue but not necessarily for your health.

The worst cases I've seen are contractors who start early, with no breakfast, drink copious amounts of coffee and/or tea during the day, miss lunch, snack on chocolate and crisps constantly during the day, work at their desk, with bad posture or are on the phone constantly and never take a break, slump during meetings, leave work late and go for a pub dinner including dessert (because they're so hungry!), wash it down with a few pints, go to bed and do all again the next day. It's the easiest recipe for piling on a load of weight and becoming really unfit and it will catch up with you!

Be warned, this could be **YOU!** It takes effort to ensure you keep fit and don't spend all your time at work. It's easy to get sucked into it, especially as the client realises your value and places more responsibility with you.

So here are some top tips for looking after yourself.

10 Tips for looking after your diet
1. Do eat regularly – don't miss meals and do eat breakfast
2. Do avoid lots of easy microwave dinners – they are full of fat!
3. Do eat plenty of vegetables and fruit – 5 a day – keep fruit on your desk – you will eat it and it stops you snacking
4. Do drink water regularly throughout the day – have a bottle of water on your desk (get through 2 litres of water a day)
5. Do eat a balanced diet
6. Don't snack! - other than on fruit/veg
7. Don't drink too much alcohol, tea or coffee
8. Don't eat too much chocolate – great for a boost of energy, but soon over
9. Don't have too much rich food (client dinners!)
10. Don't eat anything that looks dodgy or is out of date – it's simply not worth it!

Seems like common sense? Well, I challenge you to see if you can make 8/10 each week!

So that's the inner part of you but what about you in the office – you need to look after yourself there too. So here's a few (obvious) tips – but you'd be surprised how many people don't do these simple things, especially first –time contractors, trying to make a good impression.

10 Tips for looking after yourself in the workplace
1. Do ensure you have the right chair, desk and computer equipment – use the Display Screen Equipment (DSE) guidelines (www. hse.gov.uk/msd/dse) or download the Working with VDUs guidelines (www.hse.gov.uk/pubns/indg36.pdf)
2. Do look up regularly from your computer
3. Do stretches at your desk (see www.wedmd.com/fitness-exercises)
4. Do take time to regularly walk away from the screen
5. Do try and get out of the office during the day and get some fresh air and some rays
6. Do maintain good posture at work
7. Do take time for lunch
8. Do try to leave work on time at least once per week – if time/client/project permits
9. Don't be forever checking your Blackberry or phone – give yourself a break
10. Don't work too many long hours

You know you've got it right if you're maintaining your weight level, you're eating and exercising regularly and you're sleeping well. You should be sufficiently tired to get a good night's sleep but not too tired that you're waking early, thinking about work.

10 Tips for looking after yourself outside the workplace
1. Do exercise regularly – walking is easiest – make sure you're doing 30 minutes walking per day
2. Do take holidays – I know it's counter intuitive to the contractor mantra of being there for the client but everyone needs a break
3. Do stay in touch with family and friends regularly
4. Do go to bed at a reasonable hour
5. Do find somewhere quiet to stay if you're away during the week
6. Do allow yourself time to get into work – don't be on the last minute every day
7. Do try and have a regular hobby or pastime that you pursue once a week and then do it!
8. Do take time to pamper yourself – health clubs, massages, facials
9. Do get yourself a decent car if you have to do a lot of travelling on the roads
10. Don't work weekends – it's always a temptation but try not to do this if you can

And if you're ill, really ill, DON'T go into the office. You're likely to do more harm than good for the team, so keep it to yourself. Just don't do it too often – you lightweight!

GOING BACK PERM

What? Wash your mouth out! How dare you even consider this?

So, that's my view, anyway. But some people do, generally because of a change in their circumstances. I did make a move back to a client from a consulting firm (shock, horror, I know!). My wife was pregnant with our first child. I had done a great job with my client and they turned to me and said would I fancy a job. I was pretty convinced they couldn't afford me but I was wrong. So when they offered me more money, a better company car allowance, more holidays and I could go home every night, it was a bit of a no brainer! Only lasted 2 years though, before I came to my senses and went independent.

So I would think carefully about going back into a permanent job. There are pros and cons.

10 pros of taking a Permanent Job
1. You get a regular salary
2. You get perks (pension, company car, private health insurance)
3. You get to go on training courses
4. You get personal development
5. You get to go to the same place each day (potentially)
6. You can build a career
7. You can build a social network at home and at work
8. You get home every night (potentially)
9. You get a company brand behind you (which can be good or bad)
10. You get security (potentially)

If these things are important to you, then you should seriously get back into a permanent role. I write 'potentially' against some of these because you may still find yourself working at different places, you may not get home every night and, crucially, if you think you get more security in a permanent role, think carefully. You are still on one month's notice or 3 months, maybe 6 months notice if you're lucky. You get one month's notice in a contract job and some of my colleagues have managed to get 3 month terms written into their contracts. People do regularly get made redundant and companies quite often work on a principle of LIFO, last in, first out, meaning that you are more likely to lose your job if there are redundancies when you move into a new job.

10 cons of taking a Permanent Job
1. You lose the freedom to choose where you work and who you work for
2. Someone else determines your future
3. You will probably not get paid as much
4. You will have to put up with the office and company politics
5. You will limit your experience of different working environments
6. You will have a fixed amount of holiday per year
7. You will have a fixed pay per year (excluding bonuses)
8. The breadth of your network will be more constrained
9. You will be more constrained in taking up opportunities that may come your way
10. You lose the freedom to choose where you work and who you work for

Now, this is just a quick reminder of why you thought of leaving and going contracting in the first place! In my mind, this IS what it's all about. It's why I left permanent employment. If the prospect of the 'cons' for moving back perm fill you with dread and the rest of this book has convinced you that going contracting isn't quite as hard as you first thought, then I have done my job well.

GO DO IT!

So there you have it. I hope at best, you now feel as though you are well equipped to know what you're getting into as you make the journey into contracting and at least, that I've given you food for thought.

There are risks in moving into contracting, it's true but if you genuinely want to be your own boss and determine your own future, there are few better or more rewarding ways.

So I encourage you to make the step – Break Free and Go Contracting and enjoy contracting for the freedom if gives you. If you don't, you will never know whether it's the right thing for you. Nothing ventured, nothing gained.

Whichever way you go, be true to yourself, listen well to people and make your own judgements.

I wish you all the very best for your future happiness.

NEXT STEPS

Please take a look at:

www.breakfreegocontracting.com

On the Resources page, you will have access to an ever increasing set of useful templates and calculators that will make your life easier and give you a head start. I am trying to keep it clean and simple and not go overboard with masses of stuff that other sites tend to hit you with.

Please do ask questions. There is a Contact page where you can ask any question you like about contracting and I will endeavour to help out or use my network to find an answer for you.

If you want to email me directly, you can do so via:

neil@breakfreegocontracting.com

What I do is gather together a bunch of similar questions and then populate the FAQ section on the website.

I regularly update the Blog on the website, so please do get involved and add your comments.

Please do follow me! I'm on

- Facebook https://www.facebook.com/breakfreegocontracting
- LinkedIn www.linkedin.com/pub/neil-goudge/4/35a/107
- and Twitter @gocontracting

I am looking at providing a training course to follow on from this book, so it would be useful to have your thoughts and feedback on what you might want out of such a course.

My thoughts are that it would be a 1 or 2 day course and that it would cover much of the content of the book, but that you would actually do what the book asks you to do during the course – so you would end up with a personal SAVE analysis, a risk profile, a CV (on which we would comment), a decision on your company structure, a company name (registered with Companies House)... you get the gist.

We could then follow this up with a more personalised service to hone the output and ultimately, actively use our networks to land your first contract.

If this sort of thing would be of interest, then do get in touch.

APPENDICES

Understanding How the Big Consulting Firms Work

The big consultancy firms in the UK generate around £9bn turnover annually. It is a huge business and one they are not going to let go of quickly. They are all deeply competitive and very smart. They get the best jobs, the largest jobs, global jobs, charging millions of pounds per contract. They employ very highly skilled people, who are usually very intelligent. They train their people to be great all-rounder's, skilled in specific areas but with a broad reach right across the business spectrum. Their strength lies in their size – they are huge. The biggest players are Deloitte, IBM, Price Waterhouse Coopers (PwC), Accenture and Ernst & Young. The biggest firm in Europe is Accenture and they have over 250,000 people in 120 countries worldwide. Their brand is synonymous with the best consulting in the world. In 2012, their turnover was US$28bn. And for 18 months, I worked with them as an employee on a temporary contract. They are a complete meritocracy – you do extraordinary things for a client, you go shooting up the ladder. It is an intensely competitive environment. You play the game well and you will do well.

In consulting firms, the rewards can be substantial, especially when you make it to Senior Executive/Partner level.

Level	Charge out rate	Utilisation Target	Basic Salary Band*	Salary with Benefits + Bonuses*
Associate/Junior Consultant	£600 - £800	90%	£37,005	£42,507
Consultant	£800 - £1200	80%	N/A	N/A
Senior Consultant	£1000 - £1500	60%	£54,649	£65,412
Managing Consultant	£1200 - £2000	40%	£68,839	£81,895
Principal/Executive Consultant	£1800 - £2500	20%	£93,613	£115,245
Senior Executive/Partner	Over £3000	Up to 20%	£124,596	£167,950

(Source: Salary Benchmarking Report 2011/12 Top Consultant.com)*

Individuals are paid a good basic salary and are incentivised to do well with the promise of a decent bonus at the end of the year. This can easily be 20% - 30% of salary and there are means of being able to reward above and beyond this for exceptional delivery. Consultants are measured on 'utilisation'. This is simply the number of days they do chargeable work for a client divided by the number of days available to do chargeable work in a year (which excludes holidays and training). When consultants start, they can be expected to charge out 9 days out of every 10 – 90% utilisation! This is quite hard to achieve if you are moving several times between clients (it amounts to a mere 20 days non-chargeable a year!!). When consultants aren't charging for work and are not on holiday or training, then they are referred to as being 'on the bench'. If you stay on the bench too long, you can easily incur the wrath of the senior managers and partners and score your first consulting CLM (Career Limiting Move!!). Partners don't mind seeing you early in the morning, before a chargeable day or late in the evening, after a chargeable day. For some, this is just the way of life. If you want to get on, you have to be seen to be delivering exceptional outcomes for your clients *and* delivering substantially *within* the firm. There is an enormous pressure on everyone to deliver - 'Promise what you're going to do, then deliver what you promised' even if it means working ridiculous hours to achieve it.

Partners in these big firms can and do earn considerably more than indicated in the survey above. PwC announced an average partner profit of £759,000, the highest across the Big 4 for that year. It does demonstrate that in some parts of the consultancy world, individuals are earning in excess of £1m each year!

Clients buy these big firms because they feel they are going to get a team of people that will work their backsides off to deliver for them. The client can and does impose ridiculously ambitious timescales, in the full knowledge that they are committing dozens if not hundreds of people to a life of 18 hour days, weekend working, last minute holiday cancellations and zero training! It's a tough game.

The big boys have a presence in every large company in the UK. They have often been the incumbent consultants for years, building up relationships with key people and winning bid after bid for new work. You would be truly staggered by the amount of fee revenue these guys generate. It's millions and millions every year off each client account. They employ teams of people to schmooze their way into clients and stay there. Quite often, there are several of the top consultancies in each organisation. My current client has all 5 of the top guys on their premises every day. The competition between firms is intense. But, most of the time, there is enough work to go around all of them.

It's important that you know how these guys work if you come across them. You can work with them very successfully or they can work to get you out. Forewarned is forearmed.

Detailed Tax Calculations - Comparison of Salary v Day Rate

This is a summary of the tax calculations to show how you convert a salary for a permanent employee into an equivalent day rate for a contractor.

Calculations for a Permanent Employee

Example for £50,000 salary

Summary as a permanent employee:

Income Details	
Salary	£50,000
Tax Code	944L
Tax Calculations	
PAYE	£9,818 (see next section)
Employees NI	£4,214 (see next section)
Personal Income (after Taxes)	
Net Annual Income	£35,966
Net Monthly Income	**£2,997**

Detailed Tax Calculations for a Permanent Employee

a. Income Tax (PAYE)

Band	Rate	Lower Limit	Upper Limit	Tax
Basic Rate	20%	£0	£32,010	£6,402
Higher Rate	40%	£32,010	£150,000	£3,416
Additional Rate	45%	£150,000	-	£0
			Total Tax	**£9,818**

b. Employees NI

Band	Rate	Lower Limit	Upper Limit	NI
Primary Threshold	0%	0	£149	0
Rate below upper earnings	12%	£149	£797	£4,043
Rate above upper earnings	2%	£797	-	£171
			Total NI	**£4,214**

Calculations for a Contractor

Summary as a contractor:

Income Details	
Rate/day (calculated to give same monthly income as for a permanent employee after deductions)	£216
Days/year (44 weeks)	220 days
Salary (minimum to lessen tax/NI)	£8,000
Expenses	£3,000
Pension contribution	£0
Other Income	£0
Tax Code	944L
Dividends paid (max)	100%
Company Income	
Contract Revenue	£47,625
Other Income	£0
Total Revenue	£47,625
Company Expenditure	
Expenses	£3,000
Employers NI on salary	£41 (see next section)
Salary	£8,000
Pension Contributions	£0
Total Expenditure	£11,041
Company Profit	£36,583
Corporation Tax	£7,316 (see next section)

Distributed Profits (Dividends)	£29,266
Tax Calculations	
Taxable Income (salary + net dividend)	£37,266
Employees NI	£30 (see next section)
PAYE	£0 (see next section)
Tax on Dividends	£0 (see next section)
Net Annual Income	£37,236
Net Monthly Income	**£3,103**

Detailed Tax Calculations for a Contractor

a. Income Tax (PAYE)

Band	Rate	Lower Limit	Upper Limit	Tax
Basic Rate	20%	£0	£32,010	£0
Higher Rate	40%	£32,10	£150,000	£0
Additional Rate	45%	£150,000	-	£0
			Total Tax	**£0**

b. Employees NI

Band	Rate	Lower Limit	Upper Limit	NI
Primary Threshold	0%	0	£149	0
Rate below upper earnings	12%	£149	£797	£30
Rate above upper earnings	2%	£797	-	£0
			Total NI	**£30**

c.   Employers NI

Band	Rate	Lower Limit	Upper Limit	NI
Secondary Class 1 Rate	13.8%	£148	-	£41
			Total NI	**£41**

d.   Corporation Tax

Band	Rate	Lower Limit	Upper Limit	Tax
Small Profits Rate	20%	0	£300,000	£7,316
Marginal Relief	3/400	£300,000	£1,500,000	£0
Main Rate	23%	£150,000	-	£0
			Total NI	**£7,316**

e.   Dividend Payment

Salary	£8,000
Net Dividend	£29,266
Gross Up Dividend (10/9 x Dividend)	£32,518
Tax Code	944L
Taxable Income (gross dividend + salary + allowance)	£31,069
Amount subject to tax (upper limit £32,010 – see below)	£0
Total Tax	**£0**

Dividend Tax Thresholds

Band	Rate	Lower Limit	Upper Limit	Tax
Small Profits Rate	10%	0	£32,010	£0
Higher Rate	32.5%	£32,010	£150,000	£0
Additional Rate	37.5%	£150,000	-	£0

Good Sources of Advice

Mind Tools - www.mindtools.com

This is a great website with lots of resources on it. In particular, I liked the way in which they made Goal Setting so simple. They look at personal goals, from a lifetime perspective, which is exactly what you need as a contractor, when you're starting out. It's important for you to understand how contracting is going to move you towards your goals and you might realise that this is just a stepping stone to where you really want to be.

Human Metrics - www.humanmetrics.com

This is a great free way of checking out your personality profile based on the Jung Typology Test, which is similar to the Myers-Briggs test. In 72 questions, it can work out your profile but the best bit is there is a load of free follow up analysis on your personality type. The most common profile for contractors are ENFJ, ENTP, ENTJ, **ESTJ (most prolific),** ESFJ and ESTP. If you're one of these, you may just be cut out for contracting!

Similar Minds – www.similarminds.com

Psych Test – www.psychtests.com

More good personality profiling websites. They have masses of free profiling tests you can take. Remember, there's no right or wrong answer with these tests. It's just about trying to understand a little bit more about who you are and what makes you tick.

Jobserve – www.jobserve.com

My favourite job searching site, mainly because of the .csv file that you can download into excel and play around with to sift on filtered criteria. It makes life a lot easier

Jobsite – www.jobsite.com

TotalJobs – www.totaljobs.com

Monster – www.monster.co.uk

All great job hunting websites that give you daily downloads to your email.

Business Structures -

https://www.gov.uk/business-legal-structures/overview

Useful guidance in summary form from the official Government website.

Companies House – www.companieshouse.gov.uk

Essential site for understanding what you need to do to form ad run a company.

ABOUT THE AUTHOR

Neil Goudge is a highly experienced independent management consultant who has worked for over 10 years as a contractor with several blue-chip companies. Before this, Neil experienced life as a consultant with a number of the top UK consultancy firms like Ernst & Young (now EY), Accenture and PA Consulting Group. In addition, Neil has spent 15 years in line management positions gained in engineering and healthcare companies. Neil has worked internationally across many different industries including Financial Services, Retail, Media, Pharmaceuticals, Healthcare, Engineering, Aerospace and Defence.

Neil is the Director of his own Project, Programme and Change Management consultancy. His work has entailed delivering predominantly large scale projects and programmes to a variety of companies across many different industries and across many different countries.

Neil has acquired the skills for consulting by learning, directing and doing rather than writing reports and advising. In his time as a contractor, he has been in the position of recruiting other contractors for positions in projects and programmes. He has, in the last few years, started to provide advice to people who want to move into the contract world. These are the people who have found his advice so useful, that they have found the courage to move into contracting and Neil has continued to support them in their new positions.

You can contact Neil at the following:

Twitter - @gocontracting

Facebook - https://www.facebook.com/breakfreegocontracting

Website - http://www.breakfreegocontracting.com

10012617R00142

Printed in Great Britain
by Amazon.co.uk, Ltd.,
Marston Gate.